DAC Guidelines and Reference Series

Supporting Statebuilding in Situations of Conflict and Fragility

POLICY GUIDANCE

OECD

This work is published on the responsibility of the Secretary-General of the OECD. The opinions expressed and arguments employed herein do not necessarily reflect the official views of the Organisation or of the governments of its member countries.

Please cite this publication as:
OECD (2011), *Supporting Statebuilding in Situations of Conflict and Fragility: Policy Guidance*, DAC Guidelines and Reference Series, OECD Publishing.
http://dx.doi.org/10.1787/9789264074989-en

ISBN 978-92-64-07496-5 (print)
ISBN 978-92-64-07498-9 (PDF)

Series: DAC Guidelines and Reference Series
ISSN 1990-0996 (print)
ISSN 1990-0988 (online)

Photo credits: Cover © Elena Elisseeva/Dreamstime.com

Corrigenda to OECD publications may be found on line at: *www.oecd.org/publishing/corrigenda*.

Foreword

State fragility and violent conflict are among the most daunting challenges that face us today in reducing poverty and human suffering – and achieving the development goals we have all signed up to. While there is increasing recognition that functioning states matter for development, international engagement in situations of fragility and conflict has often neglected the foundations upon which strong and legitimate states are built.

Supporting Statebuilding in Situations of Conflict and Fragility: Policy Guidance addresses this challenge. It gives actionable guidance, underpinned by a robust conceptual framework, for development actors to inform strategies, programme development and delivery, and ways of operating at headquarters and in the field.

This report challenges us to fundamentally review and reorient the way we engage in fragile and conflict-affected situations. Providing support to statebuilding with a focus on strengthening state-society engagement requires a major shift in the way we think, act and work together. Supporting statebuilding demands the end of business as usual. It requires development agencies to review and strengthen their own capabilities and to work differently in today's most challenging development contexts.

Several recommendations are given to development actors. First of all, to engage better and more effectively, they need to rethink their role and move towards being moderators and facilitators of domestic processes, not implementers of outside "fixes". Second, they must focus their support on strengthening state-society interaction and accountability by working with a broader range of actors and at all levels of government, not just the central executive. Finally, they must ensure that they have the right people with appropriate skills and experiences working on statebuilding in fragile situations, as well as the right incentives to promote new ways of working and collaborating.

This book lays out how to achieve these and other objectives. It represents a milestone in the ongoing effort to improve international engagement in situations of conflict and fragility. The challenge now lies in translating these recommendations into action and generating the high-level support such a change of course requires.

Angel Gurría
Secretary-General
OECD

Acknowledgements

This policy guidance is the result of a collaborative effort by members of the DAC International Network on Conflict and Fragility (INCAF). The process of preparing the guidance was led by Stephan Massing (OECD DAC Secretariat) under the overall guidance of Bella Bird and Alastair J. McKechnie (Co-Chairs of the INCAF Task Team on Peacebuilding, Statebuilding and Security) and under the supervision of Alexandra Trzeciak-Duval at the OECD Secretariat. The policy guidance is based on a draft prepared by Alison Evans (Overseas Development Institute) with support from Pilar Domingo, Leni Wild and Geraldine Baudienville. Peter Batchelor, Bella Bird, Alastair J. McKechnie, Michael Koros, Stephan Massing, Eugenia Piza-Lopez and Tjip Walker contributed to the elaboration of key policy messages and recommendations. Invaluable contributions to finalising the guidance were made by Sue Unsworth (the Policy Practice), Dan Smith (International Alert) and Heather Baser.

A large number of colleagues from the following countries and organisations provided valuable comments and contributions throughout the preparation process: Australia (Jane Chandler, Sarah Goulding, Lyndal Manson, Mat Kimberley, Christina Landsberg, Andrew Mackee), Austria (Ursula Werther-Pietsch), Belgium (Martinus Desmet, Xavier Rouha), Canada (Michael Koros, Shereen Mikhail Vaughan), Denmark (Tania Schimmell), European Commission (Katja Ahlfors, Dorothee Starck), France (Katharina Buse, François Gaulme, Charles Girard, Valérie Maugy), Germany (Michael Frahm, Margarete Jacob, Pamela Jawad, Sophie Kraume, Claudia Pragua, Klaus Schreiner, Stella Seibert, Christine Toetzke, Leonie Jana Wagner), Japan (Motoyuki Ishize, Shuhei Ueno, Ai Imai), Netherlands (Ronald Wormgoor), Norway (Eva Helene Østbye), OECD (Rory Keane, Robin Ogilvy, Asbjorn Wee), Portugal (Manuela Ferreira), Sweden (Henrik Hammargren), Switzerland (Cristina Hoyos), UNDP (Peter Batchelor, Sylvia Fletcher, Patrick Keuleers, Eugenia Piza-Lopez), United Kingdom (Jane Alexander, Bella Bird, Michelle Law, Susan Loughhead, Timothy Othieno, Alex Stevens, Alan Whaites, Tim Williams), United States (Rachel Locke, Summer Lopez, Jessica O'Connor, Kirby Reiling, Amber Ussery, Tjip Walker), World Bank (Christina Biebesheimer, William Byrd, Greg Ellis, Alastair J. McKechnie, Stephen Ndegwa).

The development of the guidance has benefitted from comments by an independent expert group consisting of Derick W. Brinkerhoff (Research Triangle Institute), David Carment (Carleton University), Dr. Gwinyayi Albert Dzinesa (Centre for Conflict Resolution), Henry Ivarature (Pacific Islands Forum Secretariat), Jörn Grävingholt (German Development Institute), Sylvia Fletcher (UNDP Iraq), Sue Ingram, Paul Lundberg (UNDP Afghanistan), James Putzel (London School of Economics), Sue Unsworth (the Policy Practice), Thierry Vircoulon (Institut français des relations internationales) and Vanessa Wyeth (International Peace Institute). Valuable feedback was also provided by Stephen Brown (University of Ottawa), Alina Rocha Menocal (Overseas Development Institute), Sarah Noble (Interpeace), Tim Sisk (Denver University), NATO International Staff, and members of the UNECHA Working Group.

Sarah Cramer, Isabel Huber and Joshua Rogers provided invaluable editorial assistance and Stephanie Coic contributed to the graphic design.

Table of contents

Table

Boxes

Part I

Part II

Figure

Executive Summary

Effective states matter for development. This book provides guidance to policy makers and programme managers. It addresses the specific challenges of statebuilding in conflict-affected or fragile situations where the lives and livelihoods of millions of people are at stake. Fragile and conflict-affected states are those that have weak capacity to carry out basic functions of governing their population and territory, and lack the ability to develop mutually constructive and reinforcing relations with society.

Fragility, conflict and violence are not the same but they can exist concurrently, with each shaping and being shaped by the other. Thus, the process of statebuilding will often develop alongside, as part of and in a mutually supportive relationship with peacebuilding, with both processes supported by a range of external actors that includes the international development community.

Conceptual frameworks on statebuilding in fragile situations build from three main propositions:

- Statebuilding needs to be understood in the context of state-society relations; the evolution of a state's relationship with society is at the heart of statebuilding.
- Statebuilding is a deeply political process, and understanding the context – especially what is perceived as legitimate in a specific context – is crucial if international support is to be useful.
- Statebuilding is first and foremost an endogenous process; there are therefore limits as to what the international community can and should do.

Finally, statebuilding processes at the start of the new millennium are deeply enmeshed in broader global processes that can enable or constrain statebuilding.

The challenge now lies in translating these propositions into guidance for action by policy makers and practitioners.

The conceptual framework

To broaden understanding of the dynamics of statebuilding, this guidance focuses on three critical aspects of state-society relations that influence the resilience or fragility of states. These aspects should also be understood to exist within a larger regional and global policy environment and to operate at multiple levels – national and sub-national – within the domestic polity. The three dimensions are:

- *The political settlement*, which reflects the implicit or explicit agreement (among elites principally) on the "rules of the game", power distribution and the *political processes* through which state and society are connected.

- *The capability and responsiveness of the state* to effectively fulfil its principal functions and provide key services.
- *Broad social expectations and perceptions* about what the state should do, what the terms of the state-society relationship should be, and the *ability of society to articulate demands* that are "heard".

At the heart of the interaction between these three dimensions lies the matter of legitimacy, which provides the basis for rule by primarily non-coercive means (OECD, 2010a). States derive legitimacy from multiple sources that may coexist and/or compete. In fragile settings legitimacy may be a highly contested notion, with multiple and conflicting sources of legitimacy competing for space. Understanding the sources of legitimacy must be central to external interventions in statebuilding efforts.

Although statebuilding is not a linear process, securing physical control over a territory and a basic political settlement are necessary to create the conditions for building state capacity to deliver public goods, and accountability and responsiveness to a broader range of citizens.

From framework to practice

Understanding these statebuilding processes and the context in which they take place must be the starting point for any international engagement and support. This raises a number of challenges and opportunities for the way the international community works and engages in fragile and conflict-affected contexts.

Making strategic choices and defining overall objectives

A practical challenge is that the endogenous nature of the statebuilding process places inevitable limits on the scope for external action and support. This requires realism and a clear assessment of the relevance, added-value and potential harm of international engagement in each country context.

The process is neither linear nor short-term, and both domestic and international actors are faced with multiple and often competing priorities and objectives. There may be tensions between statebuilding objectives and other objectives of international actors (including a development partner's* own security, or commercial or political concerns). There may also be tensions between the endogenous process of statebuilding and a normative, internationally supported (democratic) agenda; and between short-term objectives and longer-term objectives. These tensions and trade-offs need to be recognised and actively managed.

Development partners will need to engage with a broad range of state and non-state partners and work at multiple levels of government. Understanding the interface between different levels of government and between state and non-state actors is fundamental to building more effective state-society interaction. Currently development partners often limit their support to an overly narrow range of state and non-state actors.

Statebuilding involves the complex interplay of interests relating to security, political concerns, and economic and social development. Thus, external actors need to adopt a

* "Development partner" is the term this publication uses for representatives of donor countries, bilateral and multilateral agencies and global programmes engaged in development co-operation activities and policy dialogue at country level.

whole-of-government approach. This requires development partners to develop a common strategic vision and shared objectives or strategies for engagement across government (or organisation). Joint assessments and/or joint financing and staffing mechanisms are key elements to make a coherent, co-ordinated and complementary approach operational.

Global and regional factors can cause instability and fragility, and seriously undermine the creation of effective public authority at the country level. International actors therefore need to be aware of these external factors and, as appropriate, link actions at the country level with international actions to tackle tax evasion, money laundering, the arms trade, illicit or irresponsible extraction of natural resources, corruption and terrorist financing, and international regulation of narcotics. This creates opportunities to combine country-level support with action through "third parties" – regional organisations and/or new international policy frameworks – which addresses the wider set of incentives affecting domestic statebuilding efforts.

Designing and delivering country programmes

Statebuilding involves the ongoing negotiation of an unwritten contract between the state and society. The international community must be alert to the way their actions can strengthen or undermine constructive state-society engagement. This requires making context-specific judgements about most appropriate ways to support both state and non-state actors at national and local levels, and facilitating effective interactions between state and society. This could be approached by:

- Identifying the underlying causes of violent conflict and fragility, as well as factors that can build peace, and supporting local conflict management and resolution mechanisms.
- Looking for opportunities to promote inclusive political settlements and political processes that strengthen state-society interaction and accountability at all levels.
- Prioritising support for state functions that are strategically important for statebuilding. The key functions to focus on are security and justice, revenue and expenditure management, economic development – especially job creation – and service delivery. Detailed priorities within these key areas always need to be formulated on the basis of the specific country context.

In all of these interventions it is important to place gender considerations among the core concerns. Apart from their normative importance, a gender-sensitive approach can enhance the effectiveness and sustainability of interventions in each of the three areas above.

Choosing tools for analysis and monitoring

Solid analysis is a key precondition for effective interventions that do no harm. Development partners should make use of the full range of analytical tools available to better understand political context, and the factors that help explain state fragility, the causes of violent conflict and the potential to support statebuilding. Analysis should not only focus on assessing problems and gaps but also look at possible drivers of stability and peace and institutional strengths. Even in the most fragile contexts, functioning institutions and capacities exist and can help in defining and implementing strategies.

Development partners will need to embed analysis in a wider set of organisational principles about learning and integrating knowledge into practice. Such a "culture of analysis" and systematic approaches to feed findings from analysis into programming are critical to ensure strategies, programmes and day-to-day implementation are informed by contextual information.

Monitoring the impact of statebuilding interventions and measuring progress is essential for the accountability of development partner governments toward their citizens. At the same time, defining goals, setting timelines, and establishing performance benchmarks represent political commitments and need to be appropriate to the context. Monitoring and evaluation indicators need to account for the long time frames involved in any fragile or conflict-affected setting and should, where possible, seek to evaluate statebuilding outcomes rather than focus narrowly on activities.

Adapting aid delivery modalities and technical assistance

External actors face difficult choices between supporting key state functions and meeting urgent needs, in an effort to create sustainable systems and practices to underpin longer-term state capacity. These decisions are reflected in the choices development partners make between different aid instruments at their disposal.

As a first step, external actors need to understand how aid modalities and other instruments impact the statebuilding process, and match these modalities to intervention objectives. While each situation will most likely require a variety of aid instruments, international actors should increase the use of jointly managed and pooled funds as a means to provide aligned and harmonised financial support. External actors should also seek to increase the proportion of sector-wide and programme-based approaches, and extend their use beyond service delivery programmes.

There are many challenges associated with providing technical assistance (TA) in fragile situations, where the conditions needed to make TA work tend to be weak or absent. This requires a long-term vision of where TA personnel fit into the change agenda, embedding TA in national structures as quickly as possible, and developing state capacity to manage and co-ordinate TA.

Improving development partner operations

External actors need to substantively strengthen their own capacity to work on statebuilding in fragile situations. This will require devolving greater responsibility to the field, appropriately staffing country offices and putting incentives in place to attract the best staff to work in fragile contexts.

The higher risks associated with operating in fragile and conflict-affected situations need to be recognised and actively managed. Staying engaged requires a strong understanding of context but also the ability to learn from failures and to adapt programmes to changing circumstances. Risks can be shared by working with other development partner agencies, for example through joint development partner offices and pooling arrangements.

Fostering coherence and collaboration among the various government departments and with other development partners engaged in situations of fragility and conflict requires setting appropriate incentives within the organisations.

Finally, development partners should review their procedures and regulations in the context of statebuilding objectives. This should include hiring and procurement procedures to minimise the negative impact on the local labour market and the local economy. This may also mean accepting the potential dilution of visibility by reducing "development partner branding".

Introduction

State fragility threatens the lives and livelihoods of at least one billion people in some 30-40 countries and is among the biggest obstacles to reaching the Millennium Development Goals. Fragile states incur high human and economic costs, and their instability can have significant negative consequences for neighbouring states. Moreover, state fragility and breakdown, along with violent conflict and other types of armed violence, pose significant risks to global and regional security.[1]

Statebuilding in situations of fragility and active violent conflict or its aftermath has therefore become a major concern for the international community.[2] The experience of OECD countries suggests strongly that more effective policies and operations will require a fundamental and systemic shift in orientation. Beyond short-term responses that contain violence, address urgent humanitarian needs, and temporarily stabilise the state, greater attention needs to be given to the foundations upon which capable, accountable and responsive states are built. To this end, it is crucial to understand and support the social, political and economic processes through which relations between state and society are negotiated and constructed.

Moving from theory to practice

Conceptual frameworks on statebuilding in fragile situations now build on three main propositions:

- Statebuilding needs to be understood in the context of state-society relations; the evolution of a state's relationship with society is at the heart of statebuilding.
- Statebuilding is a deeply political process, and understanding the context – especially what is perceived as legitimate within a context – is crucial if international action is to be useful.
- Statebuilding is first and foremost an endogenous process; there are therefore limits as to what international development partners[3] can and should do.

There is also recognition that globalisation is not by definition benign or necessarily helpful to statebuilding. This has magnified the importance of the global context for fragile and conflict-affected states, and increases the need to ensure that all domestic and international policies of development partners support, or at least do not undermine, partner countries'[4] development and statebuilding aspirations.

The challenge now lies in translating these conceptual advances into guidance for action in both policy and practice. This guidance provides a framework to facilitate practical implementation by identifying central challenges and dilemmas, and in turn showing how practice is improving. Above all, it invites the development community to reassess the ways statebuilding challenges can and should be tackled in fragile situations, arguing in favour of systematic awareness of context, and greater understanding of the way external actions can strengthen or undermine constructive state-society engagement.

Audience

This guidance is intended for a range of audiences, including policy makers in development partner capitals and organisations' headquarters, as well as heads of office and country programme managers working in fragile contexts. It provides a development perspective on statebuilding, but also highlights linkages with other policy communities grappling with the complexities of fragile situations. It is thus meant to inform policy options, strategy and implementation from a whole-of-government perspective.

Structure of the book

Part I situates the concept of statebuilding within the wider context of state-society relations and connects it to the contemporary realities of conflict-affected and fragile situations. It underscores that statebuilding in the new millennium faces a historically different set of challenges, and involves a different set of actors than previous experiences of statebuilding processes. Part I reviews the connection between *(i)* political settlement and political processes, *(ii)* state capabilities, accountability and responsiveness, and *(iii)* the social expectations and ability of society to articulate demands underpinning state-society relations. It describes the various sources of state legitimacy in fragile and conflict-affected situations.

Part II builds on the conceptual groundwork in Part I and explains how development partner governments and the international community more broadly can improve their interventions in support of statebuilding processes in fragile and conflict-affected situations. It is organised around five priority areas for rethinking and reorienting international engagement: *(i)* overall (development partner) strategy, *(ii)* country programme design, *(iii)* analysis and monitoring, *(iv)* aid delivery modalities and technical assistance, and *(v)* development partner operations.

Notes

1. State failure and state fragility are related but distinct concepts. Carment, Gazo and Prest (2007) note that states become fragile and fail for different reasons and that they are qualitatively different from one another, with unique problems that often require distinct policy responses.

2. See, *inter alia,* OECD (2008a), OECD (2010a), Fritz and Rocha-Menocal (2007a), Call (2008), Collier (2007).

3. "Development partner" is the term this publication uses for representatives of donor countries, bilateral and multilateral agencies and global programmes engaged in development co-operation activities and policy dialogue at country level.

4. Partner countries are the countries benefitting from development assistance, traditionally referred to as recipients.

Part I

Concepts of statebuilding and the challenges of fragility

Chapter 1

Statebuilding in fragile contexts: key terms and concepts

This chapter defines the key terms and concepts that are used in this publication, and examines contemporary understanding of the state, the internal process of statebuilding, and the qualities that define fragile and resilient states.

Contemporary understandings of the state

States are the principal institutional and organisational units that exercise political and public authority in modern times. In theory – and in a growing number of countries – they embody the organisational framework and the accepted, stable set of institutions that regulate political, social and economic engagement across a territorially bounded area. But in reality states do not all look alike, nor are they organised around the same principles, laws or norms. Crucially, the degree to which they are embedded in legitimate and enduring state-society relations varies substantially.

The definition of the state has a long-standing history. There are definitions that highlight the authority, institutional presence (through law and order) and territorial boundaries of the state (Weber, 1968). Others focus on the "infrastructural power" of the state, underlining the effectiveness with which key functions are fulfilled and services provided (Mann, 1984). Finally, there are definitions that centre on locating the state in society, paying close attention to the web of state-society relations defining how the nexus between social expectations and state capacity is mediated; how political power is exercised; and how service provision and resource allocation are determined (Migdal, 2001). The conceptual thinking in the development partner community has evolved towards the latter, in highlighting the centrality of state-society relations for understanding what makes states resilient and enduring.

The institutional dimensions of states vary considerably but what has become fixed over time, with the consolidation of an international system since 1945 premised around state sovereignty, is the territorial sanctity of state boundaries. Thus, irrespective of what else states do, how they are structured and organised, or the manner in which states connect and interact with the societies they govern, their physical boundaries have become relatively immutable. Any attempt to modify these boundaries inevitably creates conflictual situations.

Defining statebuilding

Statebuilding has been defined in the OECD DAC Initial Finding Paper as "an endogenous process to enhance capacity, institutions and legitimacy of the state driven by state-society relations" (OECD, 2008d). The process must be understood against a background of long-term historical and structural factors that contribute to shaping the contours of state formation and the nature of state-society relations. And it must be understood within the exigencies of current circumstances in the country concerned. These may include, for example, the risk of conflict or effects of previous conflict either internally or in the region, or the impact of economic pressures generated by global recession, debt, limited trade opportunities, financial imbalances and commodity prices.

It is axiomatic that statebuilding is primarily a domestic process that involves local actors, which means that the role of international actors is necessarily limited. But the community of development partners, and their governments more broadly, can contribute to supporting and facilitating the political and institutional processes that can strengthen the foundations of a resilient state and society.

Statebuilding is especially challenging when it takes place in conflict-affected environments, including post-conflict situations – places where criminal or other forms of violence are prevalent or where the threat of violent conflict looms (*e.g.* where the spillover effects of armed conflict in a neighbouring state create tension and uncertainty). This highlights the importance of understanding the connection between the challenges and tasks of statebuilding and those of peacebuilding (Box 1.1).

Box 1.1. **Linkages between peacebuilding and statebuilding**

Although most peacebuilding focuses on the transition from war to peace, the concept and the practices of peacebuilding are in principle about supporting sustainable peace regardless of whether or not political conflicts have recently produced violence. Peacebuilding is undertaken because violent conflict is looming, ongoing or recently over.

The emerging UN consensus is that peacebuilding "involves a range of measures aimed at reducing the risk of lapsing or relapsing into conflict, by strengthening national capacities for conflict management and laying the foundations for sustainable peace. It is a complex, long-term process aimed at creating the necessary conditions for positive and sustainable peace by addressing the deep-rooted structural causes of violent conflict in a comprehensive manner. Peace-building measures address core issues that affect the functioning of society and the state" (UNDPKO, 2008). This indicates a preventive as well as a post-conflict role for the concept and practice of peacebuilding.

Peacebuilding and statebuilding therefore emerge as interrelated processes, addressing similar underlying problems and a common overall purpose. The ultimate objectives of both are fundamentally consistent (Grävingholt, Gänzle and Ziaja, 2009). Statebuilding and peacebuilding both aim to help societies move in directions that are conducive to sustained development; both are aimed at supporting capable, legitimate and responsive states characterised by peaceful relations among communities and with neighbours, in which power is contested non-violently (Sisk and Wyeth, 2009). While a peacebuilding and statebuilding perspective may emphasise different areas of engagement or approaches, the potential for synergy between the two processes is clear.

If international support to peacebuilding and statebuilding is to be successfully integrated, peacebuilding approaches need to be more sensitive to longer-term concerns of state legitimacy and capacity. Similarly, there is a need to understand how statebuilding activities will impact drivers of peace and conflict, and to ensure that the causes and drivers of conflict are addressed and managed as part of the statebuilding process.

State fragility and resilience

A **fragile state** has weak capacity to carry out basic functions of governing a population and its territory, and lacks the ability to develop mutually constructive and reinforcing relations with society. As a consequence, trust and mutual obligations between the state and its citizens have become weak.

In fragile states, authority will often flow from a limited number of social groups or interests reflecting an exclusive political settlement that represents a narrowly based coalition or set of interests. Rather than resolving conflict among a broad range of social groups, conflict or difference is often used as justification for strong repressive institutions and limited forums for debate or discussion. Fragile states are also more vulnerable to (internal and external) shocks and the effects of climate change, natural disasters and regional or international economic crisis.[1]

More **resilient states**, in contrast, are capable of absorbing shocks and transforming and channelling radical change or challenges while maintaining political stability and preventing violence. Resilient states exhibit the capacity and legitimacy of governing a population and its territory. They can manage and adapt to changing social needs and expectations, shifts in elite and other political agreements, and growing institutional complexity. Resilience increases when expectations, institutions, and the political settlement interact in ways that are mutually reinforcing.

Fragility and resilience are neither fixed nor immutable, but rather should be seen as shifting points along a spectrum. Fragility and resilience are the consequences of factors that range from the structural, the historical, and the global, to very short-term events. Fragility and resilience are not necessarily temporary or chronic. These conditions – whether the product of particular government policies and practices over the course of a few years, for example, or arising from more entrenched and systemic patterns of how power is distributed and exercised in a society – can be altered, for better or for worse.

The overall goal for the international community is to support and enable the emergence of states that *(i)* are capable, accountable and responsive, and *(ii)* are rooted in an ongoing nonviolent and robust exchange with society about the distribution of political power and economic resources and the adaptation of society and institutions. External actors need to acknowledge that the ideal end-"state" they aim for is but a distant prospect in many circumstances. However, movement along the spectrum from fragility towards resilience is a realistic expectation if the right policies are put in place, along with adequate resources. A key starting point needs to be a measure of realism about what international actors can achieve, within a country and globally at any given moment in time.

Note

1. All states face a variety of challenges; the precise make-up of these challenges depends on the state's location, its history, its wealth and its governance. Some of the challenges result from exogenous shocks or global power struggles. They may arise from economic sources, such as the recent global recession; or from the sharp rise in food and energy prices that preceded it; or from political factors such as war in neighbouring territories. They may also emanate from natural disasters. More frequent and deepening challenges are anticipated as the consequences of climate change unfold.

Chapter 2

History and statebuilding

Through the history of statebuilding, this chapter explores statebuilding in various contexts including: (i) *Western Europe and the post-World War II concept of the state;* (ii) *fragile contexts and hybrid political orders; and* (iii) *the contemporary global environment. It also examines historical legacies for statebuilding in fragile contexts.*

The story of statebuilding[1] in recent centuries is neither linear nor even. The end point is never absolute, and over time the normative goalposts are the object of contestation and redefinition. Viewing statebuilding in a historical context reminds us not only that it has often been a tumultuous and lengthy process driven by internal and sometimes external upheaval, but also that the historical antecedents of any state are fundamentally important to its contemporary character. The history of state formation plays a critical role in determining what sorts of connection formal states have to the societies and peoples they are intended to serve.

Statebuilding in the Western World

Until the early to mid-20th century, the logic of "wars making states" drove the centralisation of the security apparatus (Tilly, 1985, 1990). Thus, statebuilding emerged in the North as a process responding to the need for centralised administrative structures to organise the war machine. The associated costs required co-opting the population's loyalty and willingness to pay for this in the form of taxation in exchange for security provision and, increasingly, for other public services (OECD, 2008b). Another contributing process was more bottom-up, involving the evolution of the social contract and who should be included in the category of "citizen" as defined in law and in practice. In the interest of constructing identities and demarcating boundaries, states historically have engaged in practices with strong, often exclusionary implications for the citizenship of different social groups (Steans, 2006). The expansion of citizenship from including only white, propertied or literate males to include other class, gender and racial groups brought with it successive cycles of renegotiation of the state-society compact (Marshall, 1950), which continue today.

By the end of World War II, states had become the principal unit of internationally recognised sovereignty; the normative terms of the ideal social contract were set forward in the Universal Declaration of Human Rights (and successive international human rights covenants). These gave rise to the idea of citizens as rights-holders and states as duty-bearers; this reciprocity profoundly influences international law, as well as perceptions and expectations of how legitimate states ought to behave, especially towards its constituency in respecting, protecting, and fulfilling their human rights and legal obligations.

Statebuilding in fragile contexts and hybrid political orders

Outside the Western World, statebuilding has taken a somewhat different path set against a different kind of global landscape. The international environment changed during the 20th century with wars being waged differently, the emergence of a global capitalist system (Barkey and Parikh, 1991) and the wave of decolonisation as the great European empires broke up. The new multi-polar world of the post-Cold War era brought added complexities in terms of conflict and international power struggles. Many countries currently viewed as fragile found themselves at the fulcrum of these larger global trends, inheriting boundaries and state structures not entirely of their own making, and power structures shaped between the departing imperial power and a particular faction (sometimes armed) of the local elite. The consequence was that society played a limited role in shaping the contours of the social contract and political settlement, often set forward in a founding constitution or declaration of independence. Even as national independence movements rallied, states were gradually entrenching their positions in parallel to other structures of authority, captured by narrow elite interests and characterised by a weak social base.

The majority of states in the global South can therefore be described as hybrid political orders. Nominally, many are constitutional liberal democracies that operate according to formal, legally enforceable rules. But they coexist with, or are overshadowed by, other competing forms of socio-political order; these have their roots in non-state, indigenous societal structures that rely on a web of social relations and mutual obligations to establish trust and reciprocity. There are often conflicting claims to legitimacy between elected officials and traditional or charismatic (non-state) leaders. The most successful leaders in such societies draw their legitimacy from both traditional and modern expectations, succeeding both as traditional leaders and as modern, even democratic leaders (OECD, 2010c).

In fragile situations, the various sources and forms of state legitimacy are unlikely to reinforce each other. Conflicting and alternative models of social and political organisation mean that leaders are unable to impose the ultimate rules of the game. Traditional forms of authority remain strong, diverse and very influential in shaping how formal authority is perceived and works. In some cases, the cleavages observed in state authority, capacity and legitimacy are so deep that the control of the means of violence is distributed among traditional elites, with local leaders having their own militias, courts, and even basic services. These situations are usually characterised by entrenched and persistent violent conflict. In some cases, state fragility has gone so far as to amount to the complete collapse of the functions of statehood.

Even in these extreme cases, however, societies continue to function, to form institutions, to negotiate politically, and to set and meet expectations. Traditional forms of authority are not necessarily inimical to the development of rules-based political systems. Dual systems of power and authority are neither inevitably fragile nor ridden by violence and conflict. In fact, the challenge is to understand how traditional and formal systems interact in any particular context, and to look for ways of constructively combining them.

Statebuilding in a new global environment

The new conditions and challenges of the contemporary world have profound implications for fragile and conflict-affected states. First, the global discourse around human rights, democratic governance, human development and human security is more firmly rooted in international relations than at any other time, and is what legitimises a large part of international collective action. At the same time, there is a belief that "the West" should not impose its models and norms on the rest of the world and that statebuilding must be understood as an endogenously driven process that is both political and context-specific. Third, the "war on terror" has produced new concerns about the security threats created by underdevelopment and fragility, which has added new dimensions to international action and a much stronger focus on the relationships between security and development.

But, perhaps most importantly, the post-1945 configuration of global and regional institutions has meant that, notwithstanding the profound weaknesses of particular states, states neither fail fully nor disappear. As importantly, some aspects of globalisation – especially since the 1970s – have had a negative impact on incentive structures for elite behaviour in poor countries, undercutting the motivation to support national statebuilding efforts. Moore, Schmidt and Unsworth (2009) summarise some of these:

- The rents from commodity exports, especially in the form of illicit goods or production processes, undermine the need for elites to engage in a positive state-society relationship of revenue extraction (taxation) in exchange for effective service delivery (protection, and basic public services). Similarly, aid dependency can undermine elite incentives to increase domestic resource mobilisation and improve transparent public financial management.

- Contemporary structures of international finance have facilitated the outward transfer of capital. Financial liberalisation has reduced the costs of capital movements, and the existence of tax havens has allowed for tax evasion and money laundering of gains from illicit activities. This affects the accumulation of wealth, investment and infrastructure, as well as prospects for economic development within some states.
- The thriving global commercial market of military and security services undermines the process of centralisation of security capacity in weak states. It also prompts the privatisation of security for elites, rather than providing it as a public good. The arms industry and the availability of small arms and light weapons (SALW) has been an important driver of armed conflict and armed violence within and across state boundaries (OECD, 2009a).

In these circumstances, elite groups in developing countries have a delicate calculation to make. They can persist and survive through predation on a skeletal state. However, they may face both domestic and global pressure to become more responsive to the rights of citizens, and to act in accordance with the duties of statehood. These pressures offer opportunity to some elements of the elite within a country – especially those with education and access to global communications networks – and challenge or even threaten other elite groups.

In sum, the global conditions and incentives for statebuilding in the current environment are radically different to those prevailing in the 19th or even early 20th century. Understanding how these global dynamics affect local power and interests should be factored into development partner support for statebuilding. Development assistance should be seen as one element in a broader set of coherent policies that support and sustain the emergence of resilient states, societies and economies.

Historical and structural legacies for statebuilding in fragile contexts

Even in the most fractured polities, statebuilding never starts with a blank sheet. History and structure matter in terms of the kind of legacies that are likely to have an impact on contemporary political processes. Typically, a range of factors will feature (albeit in very different ways) in explaining the causes of fragility. Statebuilding efforts must at least be anchored in a deep understanding of the particular history of fragile situations. Some of these factors are:

- *The history of state formation, including legacies of colonialism and post-colonialism* (where relevant). The particular experience of colonialism and the patterns and outcomes of independence struggles can have lasting consequences on how discourses of nationhood, statebuilding and citizenship are constructed.
- *Structural cleavages.* Statebuilding is impacted by the way population differences have been shaped, altered over time and/or resolved. These differences may be connected to class, race/ethnicity, culture, territory, gender, religion, and centre-periphery relations. To the extent that they have become deep cleavages and structures of exclusion and discrimination, these differences are a potential source of grievance, conflict and discontent.

- *The history of violent conflict* – whether domestic, with neighbours, or with former colonial powers. It is important to recognise that violent conflict leaves deep marks on identity. Considerations include class formation, gender roles and relations, ethnic/national self-awareness and local/regional identification, as well as political allegiances.
- *Geography and sources of revenue.* State fragility can be driven and exacerbated by structural conditions that are more or less given and that human agency can do little to alter. These include for instance such issues as being landlocked and being part of a "bad" neighbourhood, or having independent sources of revenue that free ruling elites from dependence on taxpayers and associated accountability mechanisms. Related factors include vulnerability to the narcotics trade or production, and to the endowment of natural resources which, poorly managed, can become a curse.
- *Economic development and the poverty trap.* Structures of poverty and inequality can be drivers of fragility and in turn are the consequence of the political and power structures that contribute to patterns of exclusion, discrimination and patrimonialism at multiple levels (*e.g.* state, sub-state, community, household) and state capture by elites.
- *Institutional legacies.* Crucially, this includes the density of state-society relations, the nature of the structures of governance, and the particular ways in which formal and informal institutions interact.

Note

1. The literature on state formation and statebuilding is vast. The objective here is to highlight in summary form some key features of these processes.

Chapter 3

Critical elements underpinning statebuilding

There are three critical elements of statebuilding that underpin the social contract and are at the core of state-society relations: (i) *political settlement and political processes through which state and society are connected;* (ii) *state capability and responsiveness to effectively perform its principal state functions; and* (iii) *social expectations. In addition to analysing these three elements, this chapter also examines state legitimacy and its sources.*

Statebuilding is a deeply political process forged out of complex struggles over the balance of power, the rules of engagement and how resources should be distributed. To understand the dynamics of statebuilding with a view to improving the ability of external actors to support the movement from fragility to resilience, this guidance focuses on three critical aspects that underpin the social contract and are at the core of state-society relations:

- *The political settlement*, which reflects the implicit or explicit agreement (among elites principally) on the "rules of the game", power distribution and the *political processes* through which state and society are connected.
- *The capability and responsiveness of the state* to effectively fulfil its principal functions and provide key services.
- *Broad social expectations and perceptions* about what the state should do, what the terms of the state-society relationship should be and the *ability of society to articulate demands* that are "heard".

Statebuilding efforts need to be attuned to all three dimensions, set out in Figure 3.1. By focusing only on one – state capabilities, for instance – without paying due attention to others – such as how power holders are to be held to account for how public resources are spent – external and internal actors risk at best ineffective and at worst harmful outcomes. These dimensions also need to be understood within a larger regional and global policy environment and as operating at multiple levels – national and sub-national – within the domestic polity.

At the heart of the interaction among the three aspects lies the matter of legitimacy, which provides the basis for rule by primarily non-coercive means (OECD, 2010c). States derive legitimacy from multiple sources that may coexist and/or compete. Understanding the sources of legitimacy must be central to external interventions in statebuilding efforts.

This chapter focuses on the different aspects of state-society relations, and further examines the linkages between legitimacy and statebuilding.

Figure 3.1. **Building "states in society": Three critical aspects of state-society relations**

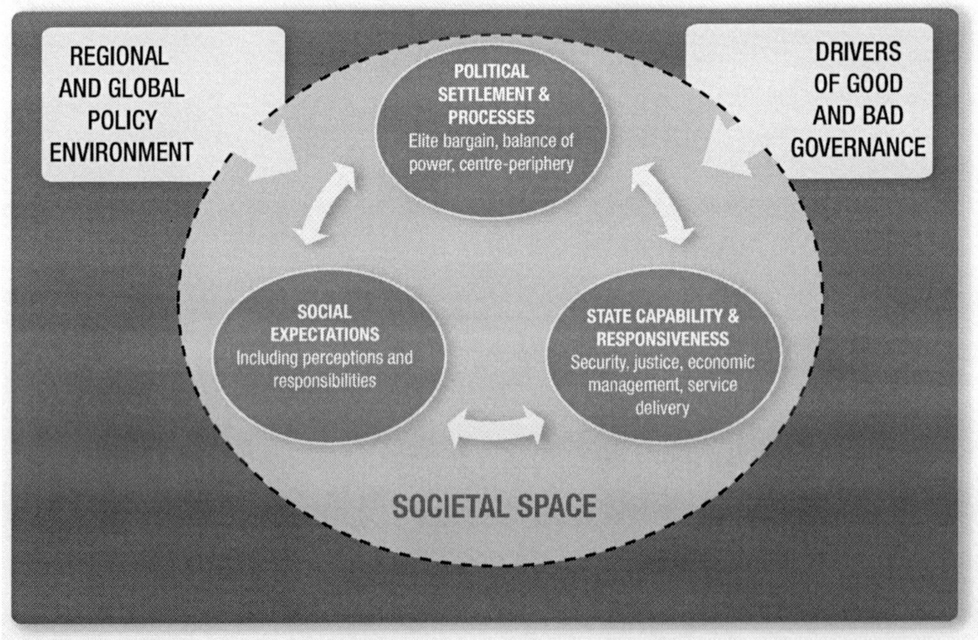

Political settlement and political processes

The prospects for statebuilding ultimately depend on the terms of the political settlement upon which the state is founded. The concept of "political settlement" is still unfolding in the international community, but essentially it refers to how the balance of power between elite groups is settled through agreement around the rules of political engagement. Political settlement may be (re)shaped by the outcome of a single event (such as a peace agreement), or it may reflect an ongoing process of exchange and (re)negotiation that extends over time where what matters is the conduct of the key actors (Brown and Grävingholt, 2009). In both cases it is about how power struggles are "settled", reflecting "an elite consensus on the preferability and means of avoiding violence" (Brown and Grävingholt, 2009),

Political settlement refers not only to the formal architecture of politics, but also to the web of political institutions – the informal rules, shared understandings and rooted habits that shape political interaction and conduct, and that are at the heart of every political system.[1] Political settlement is also a dynamic phenomenon that is subject to change and transformation over time (with varying levels of conflict, consensus and resolution), as different state and non-state actors continually (re)negotiate the nature of their relationship. When political settlement is underpinned by a broad societal acceptance of the rules of the game, it is more likely to be stable.

The existence of a political settlement, however, is not in itself indicative of the level of inclusion and participation (Brown and Grävingholt, 2009). In some cases fragility reflects the degree to which the political settlement is exclusionary and/or privileges certain groups and interests over others. In many such settings, conflict and instability are the results of contests to redraw the rules of the game along different, although not necessarily more inclusive and representative, lines. By contrast, in other settings, an exclusionary political settlement may become entrenched and stable, defying contestation for a long time. In the short term this may give the impression of stability, but in the long term exclusion and horizontal inequalities (Stewart, 2008) can contribute to conflict and fragility.

The concept and practice of political settlement is deeply connected to **economic settlement**. The political settlement fundamentally affects how resources are distributed within and across groups. In all states, wealth and control over resources is unevenly distributed, disproportionately favouring the elite, but in fragile states this disproportion is often extreme. There is considerable evidence that the discrepancies in wealth, and therefore power, are especially large in countries where there are abundant natural resources. Through lawful or illicit trade, these can be and are exploited by a narrow circle of the economic and governing elites, mostly for personal benefit, or by those employing coercion or violent force. Thus, lack of natural resource governance and absence of a rule of law can be destabilising and lead a country toward armed conflict over control of resources. Crucially, in fragile situations the incentive structures are not in place for elites to "buy in" either to supporting economic development that is more equitably structured, or to meeting their obligations (through taxation) to supporting the social contract. Instead, state capture by elites undermines the prospects for the state to keep its side of the social contract in terms of service provision, security and rule of law in ways that benefit the broader community.

The relationship between state and society is coloured by the way in which political settlement results in **political processes**, which channel the range of social expectations and political voice that represents the population (in all its heterogeneity). There are two interconnected issues at stake. First, there is the matter of accountability, which is about whether there are in place the mechanisms and capabilities of oversight to ensure that the social contract is upheld (Schedler *et al.,* 1999). Accountability structures are what bind social expectations in a virtuous cycle to both state capabilities and systems of governance. Second, political processes refer to the level and quality of political inclusion and the rules of political participation across the social spectrum. The level and quality of political inclusion are shaped by formal rules as well as informal norms and practices; supporting the effective political participation of under-represented groups such as women or internally displaced persons requires attention to the full range of formal and informal rules that may act as barriers to effective access and participation. Through this, political accountability can emerge – for instance, through competitive elections or the mere act of voting.

For the international development partner community, it is vital to understand that achieving a political settlement that assures agreement concerning the rules of political engagement, law-abiding elite conduct, effective accountability and inclusive governance structures is the outcome of local political processes and capabilities and local political power struggles, and not externally led intervention *per se.*

Key actors

It matters, then, who the key actors are in determining the political settlement and the incentive structures that shape their strategic choices. Key actors include those with power to stop or seriously destabilise statebuilding endeavours. Among them are elites, including leadership figures that move across the spectrum of formality/informality, legal/illegal and state and non-state, often with significant economic resources and in some cases strong allegiance. For states emerging from violent conflict, the balance of power is often concentrated around those with influence over armed groups, although this may not reflect the structure of relations that existed before the war.

The opportunities, constraints and incentive structures that domestic elites face (at the international, national and sub-national level) will shape the balance of power between competing actors, and their ability to act in support of statebuilding or a process that fundamentally works to their own advantage. Global and regional processes can have, as mentioned before, disproportionate impact on shaping the incentive structures to which local leaders and the elite respond.

Centre-periphery relations

The political settlement also shapes (and is in turn the outcome of) how centre-periphery relations are negotiated. As the rules of the political game evolve, choices are made about the degree of centralisation and decentralisation both of service provision and of power. A central issue here is revenue and the ability of the centre to mobilise tax revenue from the country's periphery. In contemporary statebuilding and peacebuilding processes, recurrent issues include: whether ethnic and sub-national political identities are able to coalesce behind a common national identity; the patterns of exclusion or domination that characterise relations among sub-national groups and their relation with the centre; disputes over natural resources; variable forms of state capture; and the quality of the state presence at the sub-national levels.

State capability and responsiveness

States vary in their normative basis and sources of legitimacy. There are, however, some key capabilities that are common to all effective states. States are responsive when they fulfil these functions and deliver services in keeping with prevailing social expectations about state-society relations.

To provide security, enforce the law and protect its citizens. The security function of the state refers to the capacity to centralise the legitimate use of force in order to protect the population and territorial integrity from internal and/or external threats. It is a central component of the social contract. How security is deployed will have an impact on the other domains of state capability. In the best of cases, the security apparatus enforces the rule of law, ensures that powerful groups are kept in check and do not undermine the state, protects the rights of citizens, and supports the state's capacity to collect taxes and mobilise other sources of revenue. In the worst of cases, the coercive apparatus of the state can be turned against citizens in ways that are biased, repressive, or violent, or that fail to contain or prevent the emergence of armed conflict of actors contending for political control, violent crime, and/or interpersonal violence (Call and Cousens, 2007; OECD, 2008a). In some cases, the state itself may be implicated in the sponsorship of forms of interpersonal violence such as gender-related abuse or sexual exploitation.

To make laws, provide justice and resolve conflict. This is connected to the state's capacity to rule "through" the law. It reflects the state's capacity to contain and resolve conflict; to adjudicate through the independent, impartial, consistent, predictable and equal application of the law; and to hold wrongdoers to account. The justice system is a key component of the accountability dimension of state-society relations. But for accountability to be meaningful, the law must be seen to be legitimate by the majority of the population. Society must also be able to engage with the law through sufficient access to justice mechanisms, especially for the most vulnerable and be well informed or aware of their position, rights and obligations as citizens in state-society relationships.

In many fragile contexts, contemporary notions of justice and conflict resolution need to allow for the notion of "legal pluralism". This sees value in acknowledging, understanding and working with existing informal rules and mechanisms of conflict resolution rooted, for instance, in community justice, which are seen as legitimate by the local population, and which can support the emerging rule of law. Integrating a "legal pluralist" perspective, however, can be difficult when there is fundamental disagreement about which type of law should apply, or when legal principles and practices clash with international human rights norms.

To raise, prioritise and expend revenues effectively and deliver basic services. In order to finance the rule of law and provide security and other basic services, the state must be able to raise revenue and manage it in line with social expectations. This requires a sound and transparent system of public financial management, the ability to raise taxes (Carnahan and Lockhart, 2008), and related administrative capacity and accountability mechanisms. When revenue from taxation is perceived as being used to deliver public services and fulfil redistributive functions in ways that meet social expectations, nationally and sub-nationally, a relationship of reciprocity between state and society may result (Moore, 2004). In this way, the population has a stake in supporting the state, and the state has an interest in being responsive because it relies on taxation to raise the revenues it needs to function and survive. In the absence of a visibly positive link between taxation and service delivery, state legitimacy is likely to suffer (OECD, 2008c; Clements, 2008).

Typically, social expectations about what constitutes basic goods and services (in addition to justice and security) include equal access to health, education, water, sanitation, communications and infrastructure. However, social expectations about basic service provision and the ability to access and benefit from basic services vary within and across different social groups and geographic locations; rural communities and women and girls, for example, are particularly vulnerable to being underserved.

To facilitate economic development and employment. The state must create an enabling framework for trade, investment, employment and economic growth. Enabling wealth accumulation, income earning and the development of investments in human capital can make significant contributions to positive state-society relations. Political stability and social peace are more likely under conditions of equitable economic growth and social development. At the same time, economic development is facilitated by state structures that provide basic infrastructure for investment, protection of property rights, legal security and a regulatory framework for financial and economic transactions.

The effectiveness with which the different state functions are carried out and services delivered also depends on the interaction among them, and the mutually reinforcing synergies that are activated as a result. Where one or more of the functions enter a cycle of deterioration, this is likely to have a negative impact on the other state functions and to contribute to fragility. The manner and the extent of provision of these state functions remain part of the political process through which the interests of citizens, policy makers and providers are reconciled.

A state that can fulfil the functions outlined above is well on the way towards being a resilient state. These functions therefore usefully suggest generic objectives in a statebuilding process. They can equally well be expressed in one context as the objectives of a social movement or political party, and in another context as the purpose of development partner engagement. In addition, as indicators of capability and responsiveness, the functions are part of social, political and economic expectations, and the political settlement and processes. The tendency to seize upon these four capabilities, and translate them into projects and programmes, needs to be resisted. Strengthening key state capabilities (police, the judiciary, public financial management, etc.) from a technical standpoint alone is insufficient. To treat these merely as technical exercises denies the fundamentally political basis of statebuilding, and risks ignoring and addressing the political interests that have resulted in the current status quo.

Key actors

Given the complexities that arise from limited state presence and capability across the territory in fragile states, it is frequently the case that the provision of key functions and service is in the hands of a range of non-state actors, including international and domestic non-governmental organisations (NGOs) and civil society organisations (CSOs), traditional authorities, and in some cases criminal organisations or armed groups that challenge and compete with the formal authority, capacity and legitimacy of the state.

Centre-periphery relations

To a considerable extent, state capability and responsiveness need to be assessed also in terms of their prevalence across the territory. As indicated, a fragile or conflict-affected state may have extremely limited authority in (and even access to) large swathes of territory. Statebuilding has historically focused on the centralisation of the coercive (*i.e.* security, law enforcement), administrative and service provision apparatus of the state. In fragile situations this has tended to mean that statebuilding has been more visible in the capital cities, and the population in the more remote or distant parts of the territory often have limited and unsatisfactory interactions with the state. In these areas, informal or community systems of rules operate with varying levels of acceptance, and are likely to have more presence than state institutions or state law. In this context, the traditional pattern of top-down statebuilding risks exacerbating the problem; it can secure the position of the central elite precisely by not extending to large rural areas, which therefore remain under the sway of local leaders. This is exactly the kind of implicit bargain that perpetuates elite rule but impoverishment and insecurity for the majority.

Social expectations

As highlighted before, a resilient state that is also responsive is one that is closely aligned with prevailing social expectations about what the state should deliver (OECD, 2008c). Social expectations are articulated and channelled through the political process – to greater or lesser effect. We can distinguish between "realistic expectations" and "normative expectations" regarding how society sees the state (OECD, 2010a).

Normative expectations are based on beliefs and perceptions about what a state should look like, what it should deliver, and how it should relate to society, which is in turn related to how legitimacy narratives about state-society relations evolve. Normative expectations are above all the product of the changing interaction between political contestation, ideology and beliefs.

Realistic expectations refer to what the population expects the state to deliver in reality, based on previous experience (OECD, 2010a).

There is always, in all country contexts, a gap between the realistic and normative expectations, as citizens are more often than not disappointed, either by government or state responsiveness. But in fragile contexts the population typically either expects little from the state in terms of service provision (as a matter of capability), or sees the state as the source of repression or instability, or as the "privatised" domain of elite groups. The mismatch between normative and realistic expectations of the state can contribute to entrenching perceptions and corresponding patterns of conduct among the different stakeholders. But crucially, it strikes at the heart of whether state-society relations are perceived to be legitimate or not.

Social expectations about state-society relations are also shaped by changes in political voice and social mobilisation from below. How effectively expectations for change find political voice is shaped not only by the terms of the political settlement, but also by existing levels of mobilisation capacity in civil society. Where societies are fractured through conflict and violence, the capacity for political voice and social accountability from the bottom up is often severely undermined. Of special concern is the mobilisation capacity of vulnerable or marginalised groups, which is often limited in the pre-conflict period and at particular risk of being undermined in societies impacted by conflict. The persistent neglect of structural and relational inequalities – such as the neglect of children's rights, systematic gender inequality, and ongoing exclusion of indigenous peoples and other vulnerable minorities in fragile states – is related to the absence of effective channels for voice and substantive participation.

Finally, in fragile situations, there is often the added complexity that social expectations about the state are highly heterogeneous or polarised. In part this reflects problems of social cohesion that are perpetuated by a state that delivers public goods in an uneven manner. It may also reflect differently formed views about state-society relations. Whatever the source of the problem, a shared sense of citizenship is missing, and the political settlement has not succeeded in brokering a *modus vivendi* between different normative views about the social contract. It is vital in such settings that external backing for the promise of reform and change is carefully moderated so as to avoid over-inflated social expectations beyond what is reasonably possible in a context of fragility.

Key actors

Key actors include those political elites charged with representing political preferences. Under democratic governance regimes this largely means political parties. Elsewhere, political elite structures may include both lawful and illicit elements, including individuals or groups engaged in organised crime and corruption. Political parties in such settings will have support, to varying degrees, from elite structures or exclusive economic interests. Non-state and civil society organisations can be important actors in support (or not) of responsive statebuilding. The degree to which these organisations are truly "civil" or representative varies, however, as non-state actors may include warlords, or criminal groups participating in illicit activities.

Centre-periphery relations

In hybrid political orders, social expectations about state-society relations will be especially disparate and fragmented. This is likely to be further accentuated by the political and geographic distance between the centre and periphery and the fact that different social and political actors will have different experiences of state functioning depending on their location. The challenge for statebuilding lies in working across these multiple levels of state-society relations, and understanding the range of experiences and expectations of public authority that they engender.

State legitimacy

Legitimacy matters because it provides the basis for rule by consent rather than by coercion (OECD, 2010c). The lack of legitimacy contributes to fragility because it undermines state authority and capacity given that people are unwilling to engage with the state. Understanding the sources and processes that increase legitimacy are central to effective statebuilding. This requires a deep appreciation, without preconceived or fixed ideas, of how people's perceptions and beliefs about what constitutes legitimate public authority are shaped in a specific context.

There are four main sources of legitimacy, which play out differently in varying social and political contexts:

- *Input (process) legitimacy* relates to the observance of agreed rules of procedure through which the state takes binding decisions and organises people's participation. In Western states these rules will be mainly formal (usually enshrined in the constitution), and include competitive elections, bureaucratic management and formal accountability mechanisms. In non-Western states, process legitimacy may also be based on customary law or practice.

- *Output (performance) legitimacy* depends on perceptions about state performance, and the effectiveness and quality of the services delivered. The ability to provide security, basic social services and an enabling framework for economic development and employment are fundamental. Patronage in Western states undermines input and performance legitimacy, but it may be a source of both input and output legitimacy in non-Western, hybrid political orders.
- *Shared beliefs* are shared narratives about what public authority should be, shaped by tradition, historical processes of collective identities, and structures of socialisation (these include for instance nationalism, culture, religion, gender roles and ethnicity). Legitimacy based on charisma is also included in how beliefs about legitimacy are shaped.
- *International legitimacy* derives from recognition of the state's sovereignty and legitimacy by external actors. This may also be a source of internal legitimacy, or may conflict with it: to have a positive effect, international legitimacy has to resonate with internal notions of legitimacy.

It is important to distinguish between state legitimacy and the legitimacy of specific regimes or political leaders.[2] Legitimacy of the state or regime is also likely to vary significantly in different areas, and among different communities.

Understanding the links between legitimacy and state capacity is central to statebuilding and the evolving political settlement. People's perceptions of legitimacy reside at the core of their willingness to engage with the state, to accept its "right to rule". Legitimacy strengthens capacity because the state can rely mainly on non-coercive authority: citizens can be motivated to mobilise and engage in collective or individual action that is responsive toward the state. The responsiveness of citizens enables states to better appreciate and manage competing interests and to design and implement policies that are equally responsive to citizens' needs, goals and interests. Capacity is likely to improve legitimacy and further stimulate collective action that effectively aggregates and channels citizen demands and expectations. In this way, capacity and legitimacy are mutually reinforcing, and can create virtuous or (in fragile situations) vicious circles (where lack of capacity undermines legitimacy and *vice versa*).

Legitimacy matters at every stage of statebuilding. It can support or inhibit the negotiation of an initial political settlement. That settlement provides the basis for a shift from purely coercive state power to the acceptance of the state as the highest (legitimate) authority in society, entitled and indeed expected to make and enforce binding decisions for society as a whole. As statebuilding processes gather momentum, perceptions of legitimacy are also central to the establishment of constructive state-society relations that can support bargaining to achieve institutionalised arrangements for managing conflict, negotiating access to resources, and producing and distributing public goods.

As noted in the discussion of hybrid political orders in Chapter 2, different sources of legitimacy interact and compete. Particularly when it comes to shared beliefs of religion, culture, and other areas of tradition, normative beliefs may differ substantially across regions and sub-regions and between elites and non-elites within the nation-state. Where narratives of legitimacy conflict, possibilities for widely held conventions on the rights and duties of citizens and the state within the social contract are diminished. Non-state actors including warlords, insurgents, and criminal networks may take advantage of the state's lack of capacity and legitimacy to offer alternative systems of government. Legitimacy in fragile situations is therefore very complex, with different sources of legitimacy coexisting, competing and conflicting – and interacting with other sources of power and interest. These are very difficult issues for outsiders to grasp, much less influence constructively.

Development practitioners have recognised that top-down models of statebuilding will fail if they clash with local perceptions about what constitutes legitimate public authority. This presents a number of substantial dilemmas. For instance, the development partner community is committed to supporting statebuilding that is in keeping with international human rights norms or rational-legal notions of legal accountability – but this might not match local beliefs and traditions about how power is best exercised (OECD, 2010c).

There is increasing interest among development practitioners in deliberate strategies for supporting the marriage of indigenous, customary and communal institutions of governance with introduced, Western state institutions, with a view to creating constructive interaction and positive mutual accommodation. An emerging concept is that of **"grounded legitimacy"** (Clements, 2008) as "a way of incorporating traditional authorities and practices within the formal state in order to provide the belief systems within which to enhance the capacity and effectiveness of new forms of statehood" (OECD, 2010c). However, two notes of caution are in order. First, a mechanistic fusion will not work. Introducing customary practice into formal state law or anchoring new rules in traditional practice requires constructive interaction between different sources of legitimacy. Fusion of justice systems has to be negotiated through political processes of bargaining between the state and different groups in society. A second, related consideration is that external actors are likely, even in the best of circumstances, to only have a facilitating or catalytic role in creating space or opportunity for such interaction to take place. It is no accident that some of the most successful examples of "grounded legitimacy" – including the role of customary institutions and traditional leaders in Botswana and Somaliland – were led by domestic actors, with little or no participation by development partners or other external actors.

In sum, statebuilding involves a complex process of navigating through the different narratives of legitimacy and systems of trust as the basis for constructing widely held or common understandings of state-society relations and public authority.

Conclusion

Effective states matter for development, and the prospects for moving from fragility to resilience depend on the capability, accountability and responsiveness of the state and its relationship with society. At the same time, statebuilding is constrained or undermined by the very conditions of fragility that make it necessary. This has implications for the citizens and communities that live in fragile states, particularly for their basic security, livelihoods and basic wellbeing. Fragility, conflict and violence are not the same but they can exist concurrently, with each shaping and being shaped by the other. Thus, the processes of statebuilding will often develop alongside and in a mutually supportive relationship with peacebuilding, with both processes supported by a range of internal and external actors that includes the development community. Finally, statebuilding at the start of the new millennium is deeply enmeshed in broader global processes that can enable or constrain statebuilding.

Notes

1. Institutions across multiple levels of society, such as systems of religion, family and education, are not conventionally understood as "political", but also play an important role in shaping access to and control over the material and symbolic resources that form the basis of political interaction and conduct.

2. In some cases, particular groups may reject the very existence of the state. Other cases are more subtle: the legitimacy of the state and its institutions may be high, but what is rejected or challenged is the "occupation" of the state by a narrow regime, the elite, or an exclusive set of interests. In theory the distinction is clear but in practice it is often blurred.

Part II

Policy guidance and recommendations

As described in Part I, statebuilding is an endogenous and fundamentally political process led by political, social and economic forces within a country. Statebuilding involves striking a balance between the need for the state to have coercive power (to control violence, enforce agreed rules and raise revenue), and the need for it to gain acceptance and support by being accountable and responsive to citizens. This is achieved through continual interaction and bargaining between state and society through which the parties can identify common interests (for example in security and economic growth), and negotiate ways to pursue them. This bargaining process underpins three essential aspects of the statebuilding process, set out in Box 0.1. Although this is not a linear process, physical control over a territory and a basic political settlement are necessary conditions for building state capacity to deliver a broader range of public goods, and to ensure accountability and responsiveness to a broader range of citizens.

Box 0.1. **Three critical aspects of statebuilding**

Political settlements – These are usually negotiated between elites and involve recognition of the state's right to exercise coercion within a defined territory. They shape rules of political, social and economic exchange, and define relations of power and how authority is exercised. Political settlements may be embodied in a peace agreement or a constitution, but also reflect more informal arrangements – for example, patterns of rent-seeking and state capture by elites, as well as patterns of inclusion, exclusion, discrimination, oppression or co-option that contribute to fragility. Linked to this, history matters: there is no tabula rasa on which processes of statebuilding are written. Instead, structural features and historical patterns are likely to provide important information regarding the constraints and possibilities of change for statebuilding.

State capability and responsiveness – This refers to the effectiveness with which the state can provide security, enforce the law and protect its citizens; make laws, provide justice and resolve conflict; extract and manage resources; provide services; and facilitate economic development and employment. State-society interaction is critical in helping to make the state more capable, accountable and responsive over time. State action can stimulate groups of citizens to organise and negotiate demands (for example for services or accountability in return for paying tax); collective action by citizens in turn strengthens state incentives and capacity to respond.

Social expectations and perceptions – These are shaped by state-society interaction that provides the basis for a "social contract" under which mutual rights and obligations are recognised. This can strengthen – and contribute to reshaping – the basic political settlement, and is an important source of state and regime legitimacy (although there may be multiple sources of legitimacy: understanding what legitimates the state and why is therefore key). States are more likely to be "resilient" when social expectations are in balance with what the state can deliver.

Understanding these statebuilding processes – and the context in which they take place – must be the starting point for any international engagement and support. This raises a number of challenges and opportunities for the way the international community works and engages in fragile and conflict-affected contexts.

A practical challenge is that the endogenous nature of the statebuilding process places inevitable limits on the scope for external action and support. What is required is realism and a clear assessment of the relevance, added-value and potential harm of international engagement in each country context.

Statebuilding involves the ongoing negotiation of an unwritten contract between the state and society. This means that the international community must be alert to the way their actions can strengthen or undermine constructive state-society engagement, making context-specific judgements about ways to support both state and non-state actors at national and local levels and facilitating effective interactions between state and society.

Statebuilding involves the complex interplay of interests relating to security, legitimacy, and economic, political and social development – so external actors need to take a whole-of-government approach.

There may be tensions between statebuilding objectives and other objectives of international actors (including their own security or commercial or political concerns). There may also be tensions between the endogenous process of statebuilding and a normative, internationally supported democratic agenda; or, between short-term objectives (*e.g.* to end violence or deliver basic services quickly) and longer-term objectives (to build political and institutional capacity). These tensions and trade-offs need to be recognised and actively managed.

Global and regional factors can cause instability and fragility, and seriously undermine the creation of effective public authority at the country level. International actors therefore need to be aware of these external factors and, as appropriate, link actions at the country level with international actions to tackle tax evasion, money laundering, the arms trade, illicit or irresponsible extraction of natural resources, corruption, and terrorist financing, and international regulation of narcotics. This creates opportunities to combine country-level support with action through "third parties" – regional organisations and/or new international policy frameworks – which address the wider set of incentives affecting domestic statebuilding efforts.

Finally, there are inherent risks in supporting statebuilding. There is nothing linear or short-term about the process, and both domestic and international actors are faced with multiple, often competing priorities and objectives. Such is the complexity of the statebuilding process that technocratic roadmaps and blueprints for international engagement could prove irrelevant or counterproductive and harmful. Instead, the international community needs to reconsider and reorient strategies, programmes, instruments and tools for supporting statebuilding and work in new ways with state, non-state and regional actors and across multiple dimensions of the state-society relationship. External actors also need to strengthen their own capacity and align internal organisational incentives in order to provide effective support to statebuilding in fragile and conflict-affected situations.

This part of the guidance builds on the conceptual groundwork in Part I to explain how development partner governments and the international community more broadly can rethink and reorient their support for statebuilding in fragile and conflict-affected situations, drawing on recent lessons learned, examples of improving practice, and related OECD DAC guidance. The guidance builds directly on the *Principles of Good International Engagement in Fragile States and Situations.*

What follows is organised around five priority areas for rethinking and reorienting development partner engagement:

1. Making strategic choices: overall (development partner) strategy
2. Moving from strategic choices to country programme design
3. Tools for analysis and monitoring
4. Aid delivery modalities and technical assistance
5. Development partner operations

STRATEGY

Chapter 1

Making strategic choices and defining overall objectives

The top priority for development partners is to reconsider and reorient their broader strategies for engagement and define objectives that are consistent with statebuilding. To achieve this, the five main recommendations for development partners are: (i) *understand the context and local statebuilding processes and dynamics;* (ii) *understand your own role and clarify your objectives in relation to statebuilding;* (iii) *consider who you can work with, and where to work;* (iv) *work towards greater coherence across your government or organisation; and* (v) *recognise the global and regional dimensions of statebuilding.*

1. Understand context and local statebuilding processes and dynamics

Because statebuilding is an endogenous political process, the first step must be an in-depth analysis of the political, historical, cultural, economic, institutional and social context to understand how it is shaping the incentives and interests of local actors, and the opportunities for statebuilding. The analysis should be undertaken in concert with the widest possible group of stakeholders (other government departments, other development partners and international actors, and country partners where feasible). However, there will clearly be trade-offs between speed, inclusiveness and the coherence and openness of the analysis. A common understanding of the problem among key stakeholders is essential and can help to identify, resolve and/or manage tensions between different objectives.

A standard political economy analysis of structures, institutions and agents is a useful starting point, used as appropriate alongside conflict assessment and other analytical frameworks. Such analysis is not easy in fragile situations where data are often lacking and the situation may be very fluid. But it provides essential insights into:

i) **Deep-rooted, cultural, historical and structural factors that have an impact on statebuilding** by shaping elite incentives and core processes of state-society interaction. These factors include the history of state formation, sources of revenue, the state's geostrategic position, and economic and social structures including horizontal inequalities. They are often long term and slow (though not impervious) to change.

ii) **The formal and informal institutions (or "rules of the game") of the state, civil society and the private sector**, and how relations among them shape processes of statebuilding. In particular the relationship between people who hold political/military power and those who hold economic power is fundamental to creating and sustaining social order. Analysis should cover how political competition is conducted, how power is distributed and exercised, and the extent to which state-society interaction takes place according to public, transparent, predictable rules, or conversely through highly personalised, covert arrangements. These "rules of the game" are more likely than structural factors to be amenable to change in the short to medium term (for example, changes in formal political or market institutions can shift the incentives of politicians and investors). Informal "rules" that are widely accepted as legitimate are central to the processes of state-society interaction that underpin statebuilding (OECD, 2010c).

iii) The **current events and pressures** to which key stakeholders are responding, including for example economic or financial shocks and internal or external threats to security, as well as the capacity of the state to cope with those events and pressures. Understanding the history of any recent conflict – including how it was conducted, its impact on different groups within society and how it ended – will also be critical in identifying relevant actors and understanding their interests, incentives and potential contributions in relation to statebuilding processes.

The analysis can be conducted at different levels (national or sub-national), and focus on different problem areas (*e.g.* the narcotics trade). It can usefully be supplemented with conflict analysis to provide additional insights into structural and institutional factors or current trends and events likely to contribute to instability or violent conflict.

Political economy and conflict analysis do not lend themselves to being directly translated into policy recommendations for development partners. However, the analysis provides the essential starting point for framing a strategic approach to country programming, helping to identify:

i) **The core statebuilding challenges and priorities.** These will vary depending on the broad stage of statebuilding. Is there basic security? (If not, this will be a priority). Is there a political settlement? If so, how inclusive is it? Do all groups perceive the state as legitimate? Are structural factors fuelling conflict or undermining state legitimacy (*e.g.* long-standing exclusion or marginalisation of particular groups or regions)? Are illegal sources of revenue supporting political elites (*e.g.* from narcotics trading, smuggling, capture of aid)?

ii) **What sort of change is feasible?** Are the key statebuilding challenges susceptible to action in the short to medium term? Is there elite support for reform? Are there local pressures for change, or incentives for collective action by business or civil society groups? Is there potential to strengthen security and economic growth by building on common interests between politicians and investors? Is there scope to reduce horizontal inequalities? Are there any significant spoilers? Analysis should help to identify existing, local sources of capacity and energy rather than merely focusing on deficits.

2. Understand your own role and clarify your objectives in relation to statebuilding

In defining your objectives, bear in mind strategic statebuilding priorities, the interests of key local and regional actors, and the likely impact of external intervention on local processes of political bargaining. This has a number of implications.

First, reassess your role as a development partner in contributing to statebuilding, and be realistic about what you can and cannot do. Define the limits of your engagement as well as the goals, bearing in mind the following.

i) The scope for external intervention – There may be less opportunity than is often assumed for direct intervention to shape processes of statebuilding by planning and implementing projects, but more scope for indirect intervention and facilitation. Indirect action might include steps to curb international criminal activity, or otherwise reduce access of elites to non-transparent, external sources of revenue. External actors may have a role as mediators in brokering peace or as third party enforcers, but long-term consolidation of a political settlement involves a local political process. Development partners can often contribute directly to financing the negotiation of a constitution and providing access to international experience and expertise (but will need to avoid attempting to drive the process or creating the perception that such support privileges some groups over others). More generally, development partners can help to facilitate shared spaces for dialogue, participation and consensus building, and bring together coalitions of stakeholders – some new, some traditional – from across the state-society spectrum. This can be an important opportunity for voices that may previously have been marginalised or silenced – women, youth, ethnic minorities, etc. – to become engaged in the statebuilding process. Some of these activities might be informal, such as facilitating personal contacts and networking opportunities within and outside the immediate country context. Others might be more formal, such as roundtables, consultation processes, and working through multilateral organisations and multi-stakeholder initiatives. To understand such different roles, it is crucial for development partners to be able to step back, work in the background and, as appropriate, dilute their own role relative to domestic actors.

ii) The context and resources available – Think about what the analysis suggests about the feasibility of change in the short to medium term, and the extent of overlap between the incentives and interests of local actors and a statebuilding agenda. Do not underestimate the time and resources (financial and organisational) needed to design and implement effective interventions in fragile situations. Given the endogenous nature of the statebuilding process, clarity in country strategies about the scope and limits of external action is key to managing expectations and ensuring continued political support in spite of the inherent risks, the inevitability of periods of stagnation, and the real possibility of failure.

Second, clarify your strategic objectives taking into account your analysis of statebuilding challenges, priorities and opportunities, and your assessment of a realistic role for development partners. Set strategic objectives with a view to supporting peacebuilding and statebuilding, and view all potential interventions through a statebuilding lens. Box 1.1 describes how the United Kingdom's Department for International Development (DFID) took an integrated approach to supporting peacebuilding and statebuilding objectives in Nepal.

Box 1.1. **Aligning statebuilding and peacebuilding objectives in Nepal**

The United Kingdom's approach in Nepal – following the country's emergence from a 10-year conflict – was to support critical elements of a peacebuilding and statebuilding agenda in line with an integrated approach. These elements included:

- Support to the peace process through joint donor funds to implement the peace agreement, and through building domestic capacity to engage in the process.
- Work to foster an inclusive political settlement by: supporting poor and excluded groups in their efforts to articulate their needs and views; strengthening new political leaders and voices; supporting elections to the Constituent Assembly; and facilitating dialogue among the parties on the management of political tensions across the country.
- Support to strengthening key functions of the state – including public security, public financial management, more inclusive and accountable central and local state institutions, and planning and monitoring functions.
- Strengthening service delivery capacity and supporting growth and job creation.
- Producing up-to-date political economy and peace analysis to inform internal planning processes and debates on critical issues such as federalism and local governance.

The UK's experience suggests that strategy choices must be informed by careful analysis of ongoing and emerging opportunities for sustaining peace and statebuilding efforts.

Third, identify and manage discord between different objectives within your own government. For example, there are often unavoidable tensions between foreign policy, security and development priorities (Box 1.2). Geopolitical concerns may trump development concerns in highly volatile fragile situations, while emergency humanitarian and security needs can often be so overwhelming that support to the longer and more complex process of statebuilding is given secondary importance. It is important to clarify how as a development partner you will interact with other parts of your own government and other external actors, and to develop agreed arrangements for setting strategic objectives and managing tensions between them (Chapter 1, p. 52 and Chapter 2, p. 61). This is essential for achieving an integrated approach at country level.

Fourth, acknowledging that not all objectives are compatible, identify and manage dilemmas and trade-offs between various objectives. Working with multiple objectives – social, political and economic – is the reality in fragile contexts. Rather than ignoring tensions between these objectives, development partner strategies should acknowledge them and set out a process for managing them, over time and in relation to different actors, partners and stakeholder groups.

Box 1.2. Conflicting strategic objectives in Afghanistan

The initial approach of key development partners in Afghanistan focused more on securing short-term stability than on longer-term statebuilding. This entailed the co-option of warlords, strongmen and tribal leaders into the government, and reluctance to attempt dislodging them for fear of "rocking the boat". It also meant that essential work on building up Afghanistan's security institutions was not carried out for fear of antagonising Pakistan or "sympathetic" factional leaders. Thus, an opportunity was missed at the vital moment when funds to Afghanistan could have made an impact, in the years directly following the 2001 invasion by the United States. It was only when the insurgency gathered momentum – fuelled by the booming opium crop – that the security requirements of the Afghan state and its populations started to be addressed seriously.

Source: OECD (2010a).

For example, supporting peacebuilding and statebuilding processes concurrently generates dilemmas that need to be carefully managed. The fundamental issue here is that what is required to end violence may be quite different from what is needed to lay the long-term foundations of peace and development. However, there may be options for pursuing concurrent or sequenced approaches that balance the interests of near and longer-term goals. Dilemmas include:

- *Brokering deals for peace versus statebuilding* – Getting the parties to lay down arms may require compromises that result in negative effects such as compromised or inefficient governance systems that undermine the rule of law or reinforce economic and social inequalities (*e.g.* Bosnia-Herzegovina, Liberia's national transitional government from 2003 to 2006).
- *Peace versus the economic viability of the state* – Economic rents, including the allocation of natural resources for elites or belligerent groups secured through informal arrangements, ceasefires and peace agreements, may stabilise the political settlement initially, but may undermine the economic viability of the state in the longer term.
- *Providing services in the short run versus longer-term statebuilding* – Where state capacity is very weak there is often a strong impetus to deliver services quickly and through non-state mechanisms. While responding to immediate humanitarian needs is a duty and obligation of the international community, decisions on how such assistance is provided need to take into account the implications for long-term capacity development and state legitimacy. Destructive dynamics can be created or reinforced in the short term, and these are subsequently difficult to reverse.
- *Responding to the claims of ex-combatants versus equity and rights for all* – Where certain groups pose a threat to peace and security (*e.g.* political elites, rebel groups or unemployed youth), there is a tendency to prioritise them over other, excluded groups, or to overlook key groups such as female ex-combatants with the potential to have an impact (positive or negative) on prospects for peace and stability.[1] This can lead to inequalities that are of concern from both a statebuilding and a rights perspective.
- *Competing or different notions of justice* – Forms of justice that emphasise reconciliation are appealing to many, but victims may demand retribution. Conversely, the threat

of prosecution (*e.g.* by the International Criminal Court) can discourage military and political leaders from relinquishing power and negotiating peace. Yet political deals that effectively offer amnesties for various war crimes including gender-based violence may perpetuate impunity and undermine the rule of law in the long term.

Fifth, be more honest about tensions and conflicts between local "ownership" and the normative values and interests of development partners (*e.g.* in promoting liberal democratic governance or market institutions, or social and political rights including rights of women). Such tensions are inevitable, given that statebuilding is an endogenous political process. Development partners need to be realistic about the scope for reforming governance without the support of local political actors. Although formal democratic institutions may be the long-term goal, development partners should be open to ways of making progress in the short to medium term through less orthodox approaches that build on informal relationships or on pre-existing, informal (non-state) institutions that command some legitimacy and reflect societal values and norms. At the same time, development partners need to be alert to the way practices, whether formal or informal, can perpetuate discrimination based on gender, ethnicity, religion or cultural identity, and to identify where peacebuilding and statebuilding processes may provide opportunities for gradually addressing existing inequalities. Judgements should be made on the basis of how such arrangements actually function in a local context, the perceptions of those directly involved, and the realistic alternatives.

Box 1.3. Do no harm

Do No Harm – International Support to Statebuilding (OECD, 2010a) identifies the ways in which international interventions can inadvertently undermine statebuilding processes, in particular by:

- Failing to prioritise the consolidation of state security and to engage with state officials to transform political settlements when they embody incentives for violence and warfare.
- Advocating systemic governance reform (constitutional change, initiation of competitive elections, power-sharing arrangements or political devolution) without analysing existing political settlements, state-society relations or how reform might affect patterns of inclusivity, exclusion, elite buy-in and conflict in the future.
- Damaging or pre-empting the creation of state capacity by channelling large amounts of aid outside state systems and implementation structures.
- Delivering aid without ensuring incentives for local revenue raising.
- Not providing accurate and timely information on aid disbursements which prevents them from being reported on budget and weakens accountability mechanisms and the political processes that underpin budgetary bargaining.
- Failing to provide support for the creation of capacity within states to analyse, plan and implement the expansion of basic production activities in the formal and informal agriculture and manufacturing sectors of their economies.
- Channelling aid to civil society organisations with no regard to the legal or regulatory framework governing associations or how they interact with prevailing economic, political and social trends.
- Undermining state legitimacy by creating strong forms of accountability between governments and development partners while neglecting domestic accountability.
- Holding unrealistic assumptions about the pace and direction of statebuilding.

Source: OECD (2010a).

STRATEGY

There are no standard responses to these dilemmas. The key is to ensure that they are understood and accommodated rather than brushed aside to meet other, less complex objectives. Identification and exploration of alternative courses of action can help to isolate risks and opportunities. By exposing these dilemmas to solid analysis, evidence, and assessment, greater precision and clarity can be brought to structure the timing and scope of action and align this to what is feasible and appropriate for the country context.

Finally, however else you proceed, **commit to doing no harm to positive statebuilding processes.** The *Principles of Good International Engagement in Fragile States and Situations* state that "do no harm" should be a key principle for development partner engagement. From a statebuilding perspective, this means ensuring development partner-supported programmes do not impact negatively on key dimensions of statebuilding (OECD, 2010a). Doing no harm obviously requires sensitivity and knowledge of context, including the system of power relations and incentive structures that motivate the behaviour of local state and non-state actors. Doing no harm may mean refraining from intervention if there is a risk of aggravating fragility or conflict, or of having a negative impact on local political processes. Conversely, in some cases, it may mean recognising that the lack of intervention will make things worse. There are no clear guidelines, and difficult judgements need to be made in each case. But the perception of legitimacy of development partner actions among governments or citizens will depend crucially on sensitivity to the local political context and the development partners' own role within it (Box 1.3).

3. Consider whom you can work with, and where to work

First, think about which actors you can work with in relation to your analysis of context and political settlement, as this will influence the *way* you support statebuilding. When making choices about whether to work with state or non-state actors, and with which ones, you will need to take into account whether there is an inclusive political settlement, as well as the perceived legitimacy of the state or government and its competence. But in fragile situations it can be very hard for outsiders to assess whether an effective, inclusive political settlement is in fact in place, or whether apparent stability and elite consensus masks a very successful exclusionary regime (OECD, 2010c). Such judgements require a solid understanding of local political dynamics. Development partners also need to be alert to local perceptions of their own legitimacy: development partner support for a government could weaken its legitimacy, if this is seen as a foreign imposition. In cases where elite interests are fragmented, looking for ways to support coalitions and alliances among key reformers within both state and society may be the best way forward.

In some contexts, such as those with authoritarian and militarised political regimes, it may not be possible to channel direct financial support through formal state structures, although it may still be possible to find other ways of engaging – for example, through dialogue or planning in areas of common interest. It is important to remember that governments are not monolithic. Where state capacity is weak, development partners face difficult choices about whether to pursue service delivery through non-state channels, with the risk of further impeding capacity development within the state, undermining government legitimacy, and creating competing sources of authority and resources. Such judgements must be context-specific, and made with a view to their impact on statebuilding, not just efficient delivery.

There can also be difficult choices about which non-state actors to work with. For example customary leaders, religious authorities, or ex-warlords may all be influential, but may also support policies or practices that are exclusionary and/or problematic from the perspective of international norms or human rights. Careful political judgements are needed about the interests and legitimacy of such actors in contributing to statebuilding. In most cases development partners will need to work with both state and non-state actors, and be alert to the need to avoid further undermining weak political authority while seeking to enhance inclusiveness. Development partners often limit their support to an overly narrow range of state and non-state actors, notably leading political figures (who are often part of the problem development partners seek to solve) and a few NGOs. Development partners need a better understanding of how these individuals and groups are linked to political networks, and should also undertake a broader mapping of non-state actors and associations, including private sector, religious, customary and women's organisations[2] (OECD, 2010c). Even if such groups are not channels for financial support, development partners need to understand their roles, interests, perceived legitimacy, and capacity to contribute to or undermine peacebuilding and statebuilding. Moreover, even when working with groups that claim to represent "marginalised" populations, it is important to consider who those representatives are, and whose interests they really represent, and what legitimacy they enjoy in the eyes of their constituents

Second, when selecting partnerships, make strategic decisions about where to work. This includes difficult choices about how far to operate in areas not under central government control, and hence with non-state actors. Even where government control extends across the territory, decisions about where to work will be significant for statebuilding. They will affect the distribution of resources and may reinforce or help to lessen horizontal inequalities between regions and groups. They may have a bearing on the extent of decentralisation and devolution of political, financial and administrative authority – all of which are highly political (Box 1.4).

Working at village and community level can be important in helping to rebuild trust and the legitimacy of the state through face-to-face contact between citizens and officials; however, this can also give rise to tensions with customary authorities and non-state actors. In practice, development partners will need to try to work with multiple partners and at multiple levels of government. Understanding the interface between different levels of government and between formal (state) and informal (non-state) actors and practices is fundamental to building more effective state-society interaction.

4. Work towards greater coherence throughout your government/organisation

The *Principles for Good International Engagement in Fragile States and Situations* – or Fragile States Principles – highlight the interdependence of political, security, economic and social priorities in fragile situations. Failure to address one priority area can lead to failure in all others. Hence whole-of-system and whole-of-government[3] approaches that build on an understanding of interdependence provide a better chance of success and a better use of international resources. Such approaches need to be considered at the very start of strategy and related planning processes.

Experience suggests, however, that common, government- or system-wide strategic visions on priority objectives in conflict-affected and fragile states are still relatively rare. Individual development partner governments and international organisations often avoid frank debate over the goals of policy coherence in fragile and conflict-affected states, in part because they are reluctant to confront the divergent motives or goals of their efforts, a problem that can be magnified by the restrictions of mandate and funding. More open and candid dialogue, both internally among national agencies and with other development partner governments, about how to balance the multiple goals and objectives involved in working in fragile states is therefore critical as a first step (Stewart and Brown, 2006).

Making whole-of-government and whole-of-system approaches work in practice requires development partners (donor governments and international organisations) to create appropriate instruments and mechanisms in line with the 3C Roadmap.[4] Recent evaluations of experience suggest that six elements stand out.

First, identify the role of other policy communities covering politics/diplomacy and military/security as well as humanitarian response and development. Recognising the interconnections between these communities, their perspectives and approaches, as well as potential tensions and conflicts of interest, is an essential part of creating relevant and strategically focused development partner strategies.

Second, clear political guidance and a lead co-ordinating role at HQ and in the field are critical. Ensuring a civilian lead in co-ordination efforts and clear political guidance on a common strategic vision is vital to effective whole-of-government approaches. Over time the role and involvement of different diplomatic, security and development actors is likely to change, and leadership and co-ordination should change accordingly.

Third, joint analysis and planning is needed to confront different institutional cultures and languages across different policy communities. Political, security and development actors all need to be involved in the preparatory stages where joint analysis can help to get everyone on the same page and reveal different perceptions and approaches before strategy formulation begins. Box 1.4 contains an example of an interagency conflict assessment framework that supports integrated strategy and decision making between government departments. Other recent examples from multilateral organisations include the UN/World Bank Post Conflict Needs Assessment and the UN Strategic Assessment and Integrated Strategy Framework.

Box 1.4. The US Interagency Conflict Assessment Framework*

A first step toward a more effective and co-ordinated response to help states prevent, mitigate and recover from violent conflict is the development of shared understanding among US Government agencies about the sources of violent conflict or civil strife. Achieving this shared understanding of the dynamics of a particular crisis requires both a joint interagency process for conducting the assessment and a common conceptual framework to guide the collection and analysis of information.

The Interagency Conflict Assessment Framework (ICAF) is a tool that enables a team comprised of a variety of US Government agency representatives ("interagency") to assess conflict situations systematically and collaboratively and prepare for interagency planning for conflict prevention, mitigation and stabilisation. The purpose of the ICAF is to develop a commonly held understanding, across relevant government departments and agencies, of the dynamics driving and mitigating violent conflict within a country that informs US policy and planning decisions. It may also include steps to establish a strategic baseline against which US Government engagement can be evaluated. It is a process and a tool available for use by any government agency to supplement interagency planning.

Source: Website of the US Department of State Secretary's Office of the Coordinator for Reconstruction and Stabilization.

* For more information about the ICAF, including reports and lessons learned, see: *www.crs.state.gov/index.cfm?fuseaction=public.display&shortcut=CJ22.*

Fourth, joint objectives and joint country-specific operational priorities help build coherence. There is no simple way to balance strategic or geo-political objectives with statebuilding and development objectives (Chapter 1, p. 47). While the strategic dilemmas confronting development partners will not disappear if government departments join up, identifying these dilemmas and managing their impact is clearly a first step. In practice, development partners need to find a balance between aligning their strategies with those of other international actors and partner countries, and achieving coherence within their own governments (Chapter 2, p. 61).

Fifth, joint financing instruments and joint staffing mechanisms can reduce the problems of fragmentation and duplication. Pooled arrangements can support integrated planning as can joint staffing arrangements and inter-ministerial working groups. Several development partner governments have put in place cross-departmental mechanisms to support joined up resourcing and staffing (Box 1.5), in order to build coherence between diplomatic, development, humanitarian and security activities in fragile contexts.

Box 1.5. **Putting a whole-of-government approach into practice – the Stabilisation Unit in the United Kingdom**

The Stabilisation Unit (SU) is a UK Government inter-departmental unit that strives to improve the United Kingdom's ability to support countries affected by violent conflict. It is jointly run by the Department for International Development (DFID), the Foreign and Commonwealth Office (FCO) and the Ministry of Defence (MOD).

In its engagement in countries that are affected by violent conflict the SU ensures that close co-operation between the military and civilian agencies is upheld, which is essential to achieving greater stability in violent contexts. The SU also has a policy role and facilitation role in taking forward UK foreign policy priorities, where it designs policy and acts as a hub to facilitate the interests of the three departments. The result is the emergence of joint plans and strategies between the three departments.

Sixth, support to statebuilding is a knowledge-intensive enterprise, requiring adequate numbers of properly informed and adequately trained staff not only in the departments that lead on the work but also across government. The simplified notion that low head counts lead to low transaction costs, greater efficiency in delivery and thus impact does not hold up for supporting high-risk, often low-cost statebuilding processes in complex environments. Low head counts can lead to deficiencies in networking, research and analysis, producing hasty decisions that will ultimately increase transaction costs, undermine efficiency and weaken impact. Numbers matter and so does proper training; cross-governmental approaches depend on adequate knowledge and training across government.

5. Recognise the global and regional dimension of statebuilding

The global and regional political and economic context has a powerful influence on statebuilding at country level. Such influence may be positive (*e.g.* an incentive for greater regional co-operation on security), or negative (*e.g.* offering opportunities for personal enrichment of elites through legal and illegal activities, and wide-scale misuse of resources). Development partner strategies must acknowledge that the global context (which they actively help to shape) has a significant impact on the incentives for political and economic elites in poor countries. In particular, access to very large, non-transparent sources of revenue undermines incentives for bargaining with citizens and nurturing economic growth. The following should be taken into account as country strategies are prepared.

First, combine support to statebuilding at country level with action at the regional or global level to counter global disincentives for statebuilding, because those disincentives are very powerful, and are issues that international actors can influence directly. Action should include direct measures to curb corrupt practices by governments and businesses of OECD member countries, reduce opportunities for tax evasion and money laundering, and change the national and international regimes governing narcotics as well as other forms of illicit trade such as trafficking in persons and small arms and light weapons (SALW). Development partners could also help build partnerships with a broad range of public and private stakeholders at national and international levels to tackle issues that require wider buy-in (Box 1.6). At the same time, action at country level can include support to partner country governments to encourage their participation in international initiatives and to comply with international codes of conduct and regulation. However, such initiatives need to take account of country context: they may have little impact on their own if more fundamental aspects of statebuilding are not being addressed.

Box 1.6. Confronting global challenges in fragile states

- *Resource issues – (i)* The rough diamond trade has financed armed conflict in several African states. The Kimberley Process Certification Scheme – established to prevent the trade of conflict diamonds in 2003 – is a global, UN-endorsed certification scheme, incorporated into domestic law in participating countries. *(ii)* Export of oil, gas and minerals provides important sources of revenue (both legal and illegal), much of which is unproductive or can fuel repression or violent conflict. The Extractive Industries Transparency Initiative (EITI) launched in 2002 by the United Kingdom is a voluntary, multi-stakeholder attempt to promote transparency in revenues paid to governments by extractive industry companies. *(iii)* Illegal logging can also contribute to the "resource curse" as well as having significant social and environmental implications. The EU's Forest Law Enforcement, Governance and Trade (FLEGT) action plan seeks to curb illegal logging through use of EU market power to negotiate voluntary partnership agreements on verification with timber producing countries.
- *Financial regulation* – Action on international tax evasion, stolen assets and criminally acquired assets is critical to curbing revenue sources that create perverse incentives that undermine statebuilding. Incipient efforts to combat these problems include: the Stolen Asset Recovery Initiative (StAR); the International Centre for Asset Recovery (ICAR) and the private sector organisation tentatively titled the Global Corrupt Asset Recovery Initiative.
- *Illicit trade* – International (and wholly illegal) trade in narcotics provides huge rents generated by international smuggling. Illicit trade in small arms and light weapons (SALW) and human trafficking also fuel conflict and create large sources of revenue. Action to reform national and international regulation of illicit trade is urgently needed.
- *Private military and security service providers* – The implementation of international standards and national regulation of commercial military and security services is often weak or completely absent. Efforts to address the problem include the Montreux Document on private military and security companies (PMSCs) signed by 17 states, expressing a consensus that international law, in particular international humanitarian law and human rights law, does have a bearing on PMSCs and that there is no legal vacuum for their activities. On a parallel basis, the Swiss Government encourages a follow-up by the PMSC industry to the Montreux Document, such as an industry-wide code of conduct that includes effective accountability mechanisms. The UN Commission on Crime Prevention and Criminal Justice in April 2009 called for common standards of private law enforcement services.

Source: adapted from Moore, Schmidt and Unsworth (2009).

Second, remember that neighbourhood matters in fragile and conflict-affected states, and consider regional approaches to support statebuilding. Regional and global factors interact with domestic factors to create a complex web of destabilising influences affecting governments and communities faced with fragility and violent conflict. Regional approaches to statebuilding can play an important role in countering some of these destabilising effects while capitalising on the positive effects of regional capacity and co-operation (Box 1.7). International agencies need to ensure that they have policies, financing and programming instruments that support regional approaches, while including strategies that allow for constructive engagement with non-traditional aid partners that have an increasingly influential presence in many fragile and conflict-affected environments.

Box 1.7. A regional approach to support statebuilding in Armenia, Azerbaijan and Georgia

Since independence, all three countries of the South Caucasus region – Armenia, Azerbaijan and Georgia – have undergone a difficult process of transformation. In 2001, German Development Cooperation adopted its "Caucasus Initiative" – a regional approach to support the countries' statebuilding processes. In light of previous (and partly still ongoing) conflicts between the three countries, the initiative aims to promote co-operation between them. It includes measures in five sectors with an emphasis on democracy, transparency and legal certainty to improve the region's governance and prevent further deterioration in state fragility.

The approach has proved to bring a range of added-value elements. Above all, it opens up the opportunity to bring representatives of the region together and engage them in dialogue in order to identify common ground and interests, thus contributing to confidence building and crisis prevention. The German experience in the South Caucasus shows that a regional approach also provides the opportunity for peer learning and for sharing specific regional experience of reform processes within a similar context. However, the German experience also indicates that although reform processes may be brought forward on a regional level, in order to address the specific requirements of each country comprehensively, additional bilateral components must also be agreed. Moreover, confidence building at a bilateral level is a necessary prerequisite in order to implement a regional approach successfully.

Source: GTZ (2008).

Third, consider the role that regional institutions can play in supporting statebuilding processes at country level. Regional institutions have an important contribution to make in efforts to counter the impact of negative externalities, and can help reinforce country capacity to respond to destabilising activity within and beyond their borders. Regional institutions have a number of potential roles in support of statebuilding, including: political mediation; supporting co-operation through security, justice, finance and currency; trade and/or customs unions; infrastructure; inter-country lesson learning; and peer support. Supporting regional institutions may therefore be a strategic use of aid and an effective way to strengthen statebuilding at the country level.

STRATEGY

Notes

1. Even within groups that are accorded priority, inequities may exist. For instance, unemployed young men may be viewed as a greater security threat, and may therefore be prioritised over unemployed young women. Male ex-combatants may be widely assumed to be potentially violent, while females are often presumed to have served only as unwilling spouses of soldiers and not as combatants, and frequently receive insufficient and/or inappropriate support.

2. As is highlighted in UN SCR 1325 – which calls for the increased participation of women in preventing, managing and resolving conflict – women can be active agents of conflict management and stability in their country. Especially in post-conflict situations, there may be opportunities to encourage the engagement of women and others who may previously have been marginalised.

3. The term whole-of-government approach refers to external assistance that is designed and implemented in a coherent, co-ordinated and complementary manner across different government actors within an assisting country (most critically security, diplomatic and development agencies). The term whole-of-system approach refers to the joint efforts of national and international organisations.

4. The 3C Roadmap was agreed at the 3C Conference on 19-20 March 2009 in Geneva, a dialogue across different policy communities to achieve coherence, co-ordination and complementarity. The 3C Roadmap can be found here: *www.3c-conference2009.ch/en/Home/media/3C%20 Roadmap.pdf.*

Chapter 2

Designing and delivering country programmes

PROGRAMMES

This chapter provides guidance on how donors can design and deliver programmes in support of statebuilding. The three key recommendations for development partners are: (i) *adapt programme delivery to fragile contexts;* (ii) *engage with government and key partners in identifying and agreeing key statebuilding priorities; and* (iii) *design integrated interventions to foster constructive state-society relations.*

1. Adapt programme delivery to fragile contexts

In fragile situations the environment is likely to be very fluid, with political alliances and interests in flux. There is often weak state capacity to formulate or implement policy, and there may be weak interest in supporting statebuilding. Therefore, it is especially important to:

- Keep referring back to the political analysis and strategic choices (Chapter 1), and keep them under review in the light of experience.
- View all programming decisions through the lens of local statebuilding dynamics. Make the country context the starting point, rather than basing decisions on a development partner's agenda.
- Avoid overloading partner countries with programs and multiple interventions, and look for existing capacity and the scope to build upon (*e.g.* customary village level institutions that provide dispute resolution mechanisms). Deciphering needs based on an assessment of what the context already has to offer is critical.
- Think about the scope for supporting positive state-society dynamics that produce "win-win" outcomes, building on the interests of the main parties as well as other potentially marginalised groups whose participation may promote more inclusive, successful outcomes. Monitor the impact of all development partner interventions on these relationships, and aim to "do no harm".
- Take an integrated approach: issues of state and human security, livelihoods and political governance are all interrelated, all have an impact on statebuilding, and all are capable of generating conflicts when the approach to them lacks transparency – which means they also generate opportunities for conflict resolution and peacebuilding.
- Prioritise issues that are strategic for statebuilding: security and justice; revenue and expenditure management; service delivery; economic development; and employment generation, taking into account horizontal inequalities.
- Design short-term interventions with a view to their longer-term impact on statebuilding. Balancing the need to deliver the urgent and visible while not losing sight of the long term and sustainable is a major challenge in fragile and conflict-affected contexts.
- Allow for flexible, step-by-step approaches, and longer timescales; statebuilding is not a quick process. Start modestly and build up towards more ambitious programme delivery in line with local capacities. Take a long-term approach that enables different elements of an integrated programme to come together (Box 2.1). Projects with two- or three-year life spans are unlikely on their own to produce much that is long lasting in a fragile context. Many organisations and activities will not be self-sustaining in the short to medium term. Programme time frames need to be adjusted accordingly.

Box 2.1. Umbrella programme for co-operation on security system development in Burundi

In April 2009, the Netherlands and Burundi signed a MoU that creates a long-term (eight-year) umbrella for co-operation on security system development (SSD), focusing on army, police, democratic accountability and oversight. Notwithstanding this focus, the SSD work in Burundi aims to support a system-wide approach through interventions in areas such as integrated border management, financial management and close co-operation with civil society and with development partners who are active in other sectors of the system, such as justice reform. Such co-operation is promoted via various co-ordination mechanisms in Burundi. The setup of the programme centres around Burundian-led project development units and joint decision-making forums.

Furthermore, the MoU came about on the basis of Burundian interest in more strategic co-operation, which led to an intensive consultation period. In the programme, Burundian strategy documents are taken as starting points for long-term co-operation. Attempts are also made to achieve maximum synergy with other development partners. This has resulted in a joint Burundian-Belgian-Netherlands strategic police reform programme. Similar co-operation is sought in other areas, *e.g.* defence reform via a potential defence review.

2. Identify and agree on key statebuilding priorities

Identify and agree on priorities simultaneously at three levels: with the government itself, with other development partners, and across government departments. Agreeing on priorities raises a number of obvious challenges, not least that opening up national dialogue on fundamental issues about the state and its relationship with society can be highly sensitive. Partner country and development partner priorities can also be influenced by different understandings of the same political landscape while the sheer number of priorities may be too great to be realistically pursued together. This means selecting the most important and politically feasible priorities as early on as possible in the strategy process. Prioritising should be based on the following considerations.

Agree with key players in partner countries on fundamental country-level statebuilding priorities, the most appropriate approaches, and the capacity needed to achieve goals. This may take considerable time and very often needs to take place under the rubric of a stabilisation or national development process, such as a Poverty Reduction Strategy Paper (PRSP). But it is important to recognise that while an important vehicle, the PRSP may not be the most appropriate one for setting out long-term statebuilding priorities. Few PRSPs actually include security and justice dimensions, for example. Consequently, specific mutual accountability frameworks focusing on statebuilding priorities that are not included in poverty reduction or national development strategies may be needed.

Work with other development partner and multilateral agencies to agree on a lead development partner co-ordination arrangement to drive collaboration and co-ordination, and to develop a consistent, long-term approach to statebuilding priorities. Where the United Nations does not have a lead co-ordination mandate, development partners and multilateral agencies should agree on a lead development partner co-ordination arrangement at country level to drive co-operation and policy dialogue. There should be clear terms of reference to deliver on this arrangement that are agreed among development partners and with the relevant government counterpart. Development partners submitting themselves to sector leadership in this way not only can radically improve the quality of the dialogue with government but also can increase the likelihood that dialogue will have a positive impact on the process of statebuilding at the sector level.

The Paris Declaration and Accra Agenda for Action (AAA) provide the context in which development partners are trying to improve consistency and co-ordination. Joint assessment tools and joint planning and prioritisation tools [such as Transitional Results Matrices (TRMs) and Multi-Donor Trust Funds (MDTFs)] can also help create a more robust framework for prioritisation and co-ordination among development partners (Box 2.2). Evidence shows that, to work, such frameworks need to be simple, selective and integrated across political, economic, social and security aspects.

Draw on local stakeholders to test out the relevance and political feasibility of delivering assistance to support agreed key priorities. It is generally the case, but more so in fragile settings, that despite everything being important, "not all good things go together". Moreover, interventions can produce unexpected outcomes (positive and negative). It is therefore important to keep testing the relevance and political appetite for reforms with different stakeholder groups, not only to build up a sense of what to do first, but also to gauge how reforms are perceived and how they may be contributing to changing incentives and supporting or undermining different interests. Engaging in regular dialogues with government and non-state partners (including groups often neglected by development partners, such as business and vulnerable and marginalised groups) is essential to establish shared understanding of statebuilding reforms and priorities as they evolve (Box 2.3).

3. Design integrated interventions to foster constructive state-society relations

This could be approached in three main ways:

1. Identify the underlying causes of violent conflict and fragility, as well as factors that can build peace, and support local conflict management and resolution mechanisms.
2. Look for opportunities to promote inclusive political settlements and support political processes and governance institutions that strengthen state-society interaction and accountability.
3. Prioritise support for state functions that are strategically important for statebuilding.

All of these interventions should be viewed through a statebuilding lens, with an emphasis on pragmatic realism and local political dynamics. In all of them it is important to place gender considerations among the core concerns: apart from their normative importance, a gender-sensitive approach can enhance the effectiveness and sustainability of interventions in all three areas covered below. For example, a key aspect of security concerns is widespread sexual violence and the destabilising effect it has on communities. Taking account of gender perspectives can enhance efforts to build trust between security institutions and local people (Brown and Grävingholt, 2009). More generally, statebuilding approaches that are informed by strong gender analysis can help ensure that interventions are grounded in local socio-political realities, while avoiding entrenching or exacerbating repression and exclusion. As noted above, especially in post-conflict situations there may be opportunities to help reshape gender relations – for example through the promotion of women's political participation.

Box 2.2. The Country Assistance Framework in the Democratic Republic of Congo

In the Democratic Republic of Congo (DRC), the Country Assistance Framework, which began as a co-ordinated strategy between the World Bank and the UN, is now the principal instrument for development partner harmonisation, having evolved from efforts by the UN and World Bank in the DRC to present a more coherent set of strategies. The Country Assistance Framework now involves seventeen of the major development partners. The strength of this harmonisation has not, however, come from efforts to achieve harmonisation itself, but rather from an effective debate on "what needs to be done", and a defining of substantive challenges to development within the DRC. Key success criteria and lessons learned include the following.

Success criteria	Lessons learned
• A common starting point	• Individuals matter but institutional buy-in is critical to adoption and implementation
• Overcoming a domestic policy vacuum	• Multilateral institutions are often a powerful pole of attraction in co-ordinated strategies
• A co-ordinated rather than joint strategy	• Clarity on goals and intended outcomes is critical
• Substantive policy leadership	• A strategic co-ordination framework does not automatically translate into co-ordination in implementation
• Effective process management	• National engagement and commitment are essential for implementation

Source: Adapted from Dwan (2008).

Box 2.3. Addressing governance and strengthening capacity in Haiti

The World Bank Institute has developed governance and anti-corruption diagnostics as a country-level assessment methodology to complement other overviews such as the Corruption Perceptions Index developed by Transparency International. The process used is generally helpful in promoting dialogue with development actors. In the case of Haiti, a 23-member steering committee – including *Unité de Lutte Contre la Corruption* (ULCC) and civil society organisations – managed the diagnostics process. Sustained dialogue and collaboration between the government and citizens' groups with World Bank Institute support helped to legitimate the process and build consensus and ownership around the reforms to be undertaken. A process of continuing exchange on how best to adapt technical methods to the country context promoted local capacity development and collective action. Sustained dialogue and collaboration among the government, citizens and the World Bank Institute helped to legitimate the process and build consensus and ownership around the specific reforms to be undertaken. The Haiti experience led to insights about how such national initiatives can help engage a divided population into national dialogue.

Source: Carillo (2007).

Support local conflict management and resolution mechanisms

Focusing attention on the underlying causes of violent conflict and fragility is the first step in addressing those factors that hinder or potentially strengthen peace and statebuilding processes. Accordingly, all development partner interventions in fragile situations need to be assessed for their capacity to address underlying causes of conflict (or, conversely, to exacerbate it). However, addressing root causes is not enough as the factors that fuel and maintain tension and conflict evolve over time. These factors need to be considered in determining what strategies will best establish the foundations for sustained peace and stability. It is also essential to identify those "peace factors" that can be mobilised and strengthened to build peaceful relations. Beyond this, development partners should look for ways to support local mechanisms for mediating and managing conflicts without violence and for strengthening local conflict resolution mechanisms. These local mechanisms may be formal and part of the state, independent, informal or traditional (Box 2.4).

Box 2.4. **Building trust among adversaries**

The African Program and Leadership Project at the Woodrow Wilson International Centre for Scholars argues for rethinking how peacebuilding techniques are conceptualised and put into operation. This cannot be done just by imposing a peace settlement and democratic government institutions. There needs to be a more profound understanding by the opposing parties that they have shared interests and that they must work together towards a common vision. Through its work in Burundi, the Democratic Republic of the Congo and Liberia, the Centre has developed training techniques based on experiential learning. It brings leaders together in workshops to address the tensions and mistrust resulting from conflict. The aims are to use a broader conceptualisation of capacity building to develop improved communications between the parties and to enhance collaboration across all ethnic and political divisions with the aim of building solid personal and institutional relationships and lasting peace.

Promote inclusive political settlements and political processes that strengthen state-society interaction and accountability

At the core of the statebuilding process lies a political settlement that reflects a formal or unwritten agreement among elites and their constituencies on the distribution of power and resources. Related to this are the political processes that underpin the broader relationship between state and society. Development partners should look for opportunities to support an inclusive political settlement and promote shared spaces for state-society dialogue. Moreover, development partners should identify ways to support governance institutions and political processes that strengthen constructive state-society interaction and accountability.

Political settlements

Outsiders may have a particular opportunity to support political settlements that result from a specific event, such as negotiation of a peace agreement. They can also look for opportunities to broker agreements on how transitional arrangements for distributing and managing political power will work, and provide support for the negotiation of formal constitutional arrangements. External actors are less likely to have a direct role in the longer-term process whereby societal support for such a settlement emerges and is consolidated, although they may support and influence it indirectly. For example, they may play a role through mediation and facilitation, working with both state and non-state actors and helping to build trust and opportunities for dialogue and negotiation across different stakeholder groups. This kind of activity is likely to bridge peacebuilding and statebuilding efforts. In programming terms, such actions are likely to fall outside of the realm of "conventional engagement" and draw more on a range of facilitation and mediation skills (Box 2.5). Two principles are absolutely critical here: inclusiveness and "do no harm".

Box 2.5. **Supporting constructive dialogue in Bolivia**

In Bolivia, German Development Cooperation supports a wide-ranging GTZ advisory programme (PADEP) on decentralisation and the political reform process. It aims to empower civil society, in particular representatives of the marginalised indigenous population, by strengthening their negotiation and advocacy skills and by supporting umbrella organisations. It also aims to improve the capacity of state actors to shape political processes in such a way that civil society can play an active role by supporting the legal and institutional framework and spaces of state-society interaction.

The German experience in Bolivia indicates that the drafting of development plans and poverty reduction strategies, the debate on a new constitution, the enshrining of democratic principles within institutions and the law and the strengthening of decentralised structures open up various windows of opportunity for fostering state-society interaction. However, experiences show that dialogue processes and agreeing on public policies are only useful if *(a)* there is at least a rudimentary mutual trust and willingness to co-operate; *(b)* dialogue is followed by implementation; and *(c)* sanctions are instigated when agreements are not upheld.

Sources: BMZ (2009), GTZ (2008).

It is essential to understand that groups that can speak for different levels and sections of society, parts of a country, political currents, ethnicities and nationalities all have a role in generating and promoting a political settlement. A settlement cannot be achieved without the key political leaders' involvement, but neither can it be embedded and contribute to building peace if it lacks active support from within society. That is the basis of its broader legitimacy. It is therefore essential to include as broad as possible a range of stakeholders in the discussions about the emerging settlement. It is important here to bear in mind the need for participation of both genders, all parts of the country, and rural as well as urban voices.

Political processes and governance institutions

This could include looking for positive ways to strengthen formal and informal mechanisms for effective communication, transparency and accountability. Development partners should start with their own operations, maximising opportunities for consultation and providing accessible and transparent information about what resources are being provided, through which channels, and who is intended to benefit. They should also look for ways of strengthening local institutions that exist both inside and outside the structures of the state itself.[1] These include formal state institutions of accountability including the legislature (especially budget and expenditure functions), the national audit office and national statistics agency, as well as civic institutions of transparency and accountability. Development partners can help support the emergence of well-informed public debate on issues of government policy, revenue and expenditure. This might include making relevant data available in local languages to journalists, business associations, taxpayer groups and professional bodies as well as NGOs such as think-tanks and self-appointed watchdogs monitoring budgeting and spending of public revenues.

Formal institutions are important, as is balancing support for the executive with support for other state actors that can help provide formal checks and balances in relation to the executive. At the same time it is crucial not to focus too narrowly on specific institutional arrangements, and to remember that governance reform is a local political process.

Particularly difficult challenges arise in connection with the timing of elections. Premature elections can be destabilising, but postponing elections too long can create the risk that transitional governance arrangements, possibly involving power deals with "uncivil" wartime leaders, become embedded and hard to change. The critical issue is whether electoral competition is likely to contribute to a more or less inclusive political settlement. Development partners risk doing harm to statebuilding by promoting elections where major political actors are excluded from the process, or security problems remain unresolved (OECD, 2010a). A gradualist approach may be appropriate. Elections may have to be delayed for several years to allow for negotiations between competing political groups and to establish norms of peaceful political competition, but this does not mean advocating rigid sequencing or accepting indefinite delay (Carothers, 2007). Viewing elections as part of the statebuilding process, taking the entire electoral cycle into account rather than seeing them as a one-off event, and tailoring support accordingly help build a more realistic and gradual approach to engendering accountability and legitimacy.

Development partners face similar difficult judgements when considering whether to support administrative decentralisation and political devolution (OECD, 2010a). There is mixed evidence on the extent to which such measures promote more inclusive or exclusive political settlements, and decentralisation needs to be accompanied by significant measures to strengthen capacity in the central state as well as adequate local financial and administrative capacity. All these judgements need to be made in a highly context-specific way, taking account of the likely impact of interventions on core statebuilding processes, and the realistic alternatives available (Box 2.6).

Particular tensions arise for development partners over approaches to corruption in fragile situations. It is increasingly recognised that anticorruption strategies that rely on strengthening formal institutions and that take no account of political context are likely to fail. Corruption can deeply de-legitimise the state and undermine the fragile bond with citizens but conversely, patronage can help build a political settlement, and strengthen legitimacy. Understanding which forms of corruption undermine legitimacy, and how to approach trade-offs between corruption and stability, are crucial. In fragile situations, and especially post-conflict, there are often multiple, competing sets of rules, norms and expectations, and patterns of corruption and perceptions of what constitutes corruption may be very fluid. Moreover, international engagement and development partner resources can create opportunities for new forms of corruption as well as entrenching existing patronage networks, while anticorruption interventions can have unintended, negative consequences. Thus political economy analysis to tease out the impact of different forms of corruption on statebuilding is essential, as well as applying "do no harm" principles (Tisne, Hussmann and Mathiesen, 2009). There may be opportunities for development partners to support more rules-based practices that could strengthen "integrity", by using key entry points (such as taxation, budget processes or public service delivery) and seeking to identify local social, cultural, economic and political constituents whose interaction with formal state structures can be facilitated and encouraged in ways that are accepted as legitimate.

Box 2.6. **Challenges and merits of decentralisation**

Decentralisation is a necessary element of successful statebuilding. A strong sub-national governance structure allows the centre to focus on macro issues such as the economy, defence, etc. It can also extend the power of the government into regions where it did not previously exist, provided it is properly resourced and mandated.

Properly mandated and resourced local government can also help deliver municipal basic services that help legitimate the centre in the eyes of the people. A strong focus on decentralisation in Colombia's 1991 Constitution – effectively making mayors responsible for local security – helped Colombian cities improve from worst in the region to among the best.

Local government is also the most visible level of government, and the one with which people interact most frequently. It is best able to respond to the immediate needs and build on the attributes of the local population. It can also help provide a modicum of balance in countries with strong concentration of power in the central executive.

Decentralisation may promote accountability for local service delivery by: *(a)* letting the principles of subsidiarity prevail where the central government fails to provide services effectively; *(b)* establishing more direct relationships of accountability between citizens and local service providers; *(c)* expecting local authorities to gather information, respond to changes in expectations, and demonstrate responsiveness.

However, when decentralisation is not supported by minimum levels of effective central state capacity, responsiveness and accountability, it could lead to a number of undesirable outcomes. First, it is likely that it will replicate the "vices" of central state inefficiencies. Second, it risks empowering local elites who are not committed to responsive statebuilding, thus further cementing local power structures based on exclusion and discrimination, precisely because there are poor mechanisms of accountability and limited enforcement of the rule of law. Decentralisation has, for example, fragmented legitimate control over the means of violence, thus denying the central state the practical ability to assert the rule of law.

Incomplete or externally driven decentralisation occurs when reforms and resource allocation decisions are determined by short-term political needs or by external assessments of the state. This approach can increase the likelihood of overlooking how such support strengthens the political settlement and social contract. Likewise, decentralisation without capacity – the ability to strike a bargain without delivering on promises – can increase local expectations that the state cannot fill, and an opportunity for local elites to then fill the vacuum.

Prioritise support for state functions that are strategically important for statebuilding

Statebuilding is inherently linked to issues of security/protection and development/wealth creation, so an integrated approach is essential. This is especially true in fragile situations where it is also particularly important to keep focused on the underlying political dynamics, and the way these can support or undermine attempts to strengthen formal institutions. The key state functions to focus on are security and justice, revenue and expenditure management and economic development, especially job creation and service delivery. One critical issue is to look for the potential for interaction between the different functions, and common interests between different stakeholders: for example, increased security can facilitate increased economic growth, thus enlarging state revenue as well as the scope for redistribution and provision of basic services, while giving investors a stake in continued security. In all cases strategic choices of the actors to work with and how to work will have an impact on statebuilding dynamics, including horizontal inequalities.

Security and justice

Security and justice are central features of the evolving political settlement. Responsive and accountable security services and access to justice are priorities for (re)establishing trust in the state and confidence in its ability to meet legitimate expectations. But in fragile and conflict-affected states, establishing security and justice under the rule of law can be especially challenging and will take considerable time. In contexts of armed conflict, for instance, the state typically does not have control of the monopoly of violence across the territory, and police and formal judicial systems are likely to be weak and inaccessible for most of the population. Several areas should be considered when designing programmes related to security and justice.

Ensure legitimate and functioning security forces. In the most fragile states security system reform initiatives may be confronted with wholly dysfunctional security forces where there is no unified chain of command, salaries are not paid, and loyalty and discipline are entirely lacking. In some cases armies may exist only in name while in fact functioning as disparate militias under local commands. In such cases, as the peace process starts out there is no alternative to an external force substituting for internal forces in core security functions. The reform process must begin from day one but will produce properly trained and functional forces only slowly. Reform may need to include support for rebuilding security forces, including salary systems, efficient bookkeeping (to eliminate the "ghost soldier" problem), and livelihood programmes for the families of security and police personnel. Such elements build the basis for loyalty while strengthening accountability. Without attention to the consolidation of security forces they may in fact become a major source of insecurity and violent conflict.

Prioritise both security system reform and greater citizen security. Doing so effectively requires greater coherence and practical co-ordination between these twin strategic objectives. It should include supporting the establishment of effective security and police forces operating through a unified chain of command, and strengthening civilian accountability and oversight mechanisms for security and policing. At the same time, it should be recognised that where security forces have previously been viewed as a potential threat to the population, civilians may be hesitant to place trust in or hold such forces accountable. This trust must be actively built up in order for populations to feel secure.

It is important to recognise that threats to citizen security can take many forms, including armed violence, violent crime and interpersonal violence. Applying an Armed Violence Lens can help to identify types of violence and design appropriate strategies (Box 2.7).

Box 2.7. **Armed Violence Lens**

The Armed Violence Lens approach captures the following elements and patterns of armed violence:

- The **people** that are affected by armed violence (both the first-order victims and the wider communities and societies that also suffer consequences).
- The **perpetrators** of armed violence (and their motives for armed violence).
- The **instruments** of armed violence (with a focus on their availability and/or supply).
- The wider **institutional**/cultural environment (both **formal** and **informal**) that enables or protects against armed violence.

The Lens also draws attention to the fact that risk factors exist and interact at different levels, from the local to the global.

Source: OECD (2009a).

Treat security system reform holistically. A whole-of-system approach to SSR is at the core of the *OECD Handbook on Security System Reform* (OECD, 2007a), and more effort is required to design programming informed by integrated military, political and economic analysis tailored to the specific conditions of individual states. The example of Sierra Leone presents a more holistic approach to justice and security system reform, demonstrating its benefits for democratic processes and legitimacy more generally (Box 2.8).

Box 2.8. **A more holistic approach to security system reform – Sierra Leone**

Sierra Leone's comprehensive security system reform is seen as an example of effective support to build the security functions of the state. The armed forces were effectively downsized and the capacities of the national police force were increased, as shown in the conduct of the 2007 and 2008 elections. There have also been successful efforts to depoliticise the armed forces and to develop institutionalised oversight mechanisms. "Indeed, the revised national security agenda of Sierra Leone displays a remarkably progressive understanding of threats to peace and security in the country, emphasising the persistent lack of human security over regional threats". According to a London School of Economics/PricewaterhouseCoopers case study report, DFID was perceived to have been particularly effective in developing capacity and giving full responsibility to national bodies: "This creation of 'real structures' that allowed for sufficient internal reform resulted in development partners now feeling comfortable with working with security providers in that country. Moreover, DFID was given credit for promoting a holistic approach to ensuring security (*e.g.* prisons, army and border control by community level organisations)."

Source: LSE/PWC (2009).

Focus beyond capacity development to include greater accountability and oversight of core security functions and institutions. This involves working at multiple levels not only by training in military and police academies (for example in human rights, gender equality, and the theory of civilian oversight) but also by practically building institutions to promote transparency and accountability. These institutions can include ones that are part of the security establishment and also independent think-tanks and watchdog organisations. The goal of civilian oversight of military and police is to ensure that they deserve and can earn the broad confidence, trust, and community support that provides the basis both of their legitimacy and ultimately of their efficiency.

In post-crisis and post-conflict situations: *support judicial and non-judicial measures and processes that are associated with a society's attempt to come to terms with legacies of abuse and suffering.* For any newly established security sector to gain acceptance, it is important that victims, survivors, and communities affected by former abuse (often inflicted by actors that are now part of the new security sector) have opportunities for official recognition of their experiences, as well as individual and collective access to mechanisms for justice and reparation/restitution. To address structural inequalities, it is extremely important that policies take into account gender-specific needs, the needs of children and the elderly, and ethnic minorities.

Support for justice reform needs to involve both state and non-state actors and needs to be sensitive to local contexts, norms and values. As noted, technical, top-down approaches tend to be disconnected from the political processes of statebuilding. Reforms of justice institutions, including access to justice, that do not directly respond to the expectations of people at the community level may be perceived as illegitimate or irrelevant.

External support for such an approach to reform will not be grounded in the local reality that may be shaped by multiple, competing sets of rules and values. Development partners will need to work with a range of local actors within both formal and informal justice, policing and security mechanisms. Even in the most fragile settings where violence is endemic, there will be a security and justice system of some sort in operation. Identifying these actors and arrangements with the assistance and support of local leaders, formal and informal, will help to define entry points for initiatives that are aligned with people's expectations and priorities, and with real bearing on the evolving political settlement.

Justice reform must also be sensitive to core values of access to justice and awareness of rights, and external actors must weigh support for informal processes against their potential to clash with international human rights norms. Of particular concern is the potential to discriminate on dimensions of individual or collective identity such as ethnicity, class, religious belief, gender, caste and sexuality. While the goal should be evolution towards a justice system that is more closely aligned with international standards – which could in turn strengthen the underlying political settlement – development partners need to be aware that existing exclusionary processes often serve a political purpose. They should therefore make context-specific judgements about what is achievable within given time frames, taking into account the views of poor and vulnerable groups and the realistic alternatives available to them.

Strengthening judicial independence is crucial for accountability but it is not easy to achieve, not least because the administration of justice is often under-resourced and closely tied to the holders of political power (both formal and informal) at national and sub-national levels. At the same time, the close-knit nature of legal professional communities, even in fragile and conflict-affected situations, makes it difficult to penetrate the system with reforms, while the longevity of the leaders of the profession means that reforms take time to implement. Enhancing the prospects for impartial and unbiased application of the law – both in the legal oversight capacity of judges (through constitutional and administrative law) over the conduct of public affairs, and in the conflict resolution function for disputes in society – thus requires a combination of political leadership and stamina. In very challenging settings, judicial independence will have direct bearing on elite interests and their social, economic and political base. While senior lawyers and judges themselves come from that elite, they are often capable of independence if they are physically and financially protected. In some circumstances, therefore, measures to protect judges and other key officers within the judiciary should be considered. Establishing links with regional and international judicial bodies might help foster a greater recognition of the fundamental values of independence, impartiality and integrity.

Revenue and expenditure management

Without revenue, a state cannot build its principal functions or meet citizen expectations. Bargaining between state and society actors over resource mobilisation, particularly through domestic taxation of citizens, is central to supporting a political settlement, and the creation of more capable, accountable and responsive states.[2] Conversely, access by political elites to revenues from export of natural resources (especially oil, gas and minerals), as well as illicit flows from smuggling, corruption and trade in narcotics, sharply reduces the need for them to bargain with citizens over revenues, to create the bureaucratic capacity to collect and administer tax, or to nurture wealth creation. The result is both unproductive use of resources and very weak incentives for statebuilding. Weak management of natural resource revenues can also encourage competition for access by non-state actors, and provide finance for groups offering armed resistance to the state.

The key issue for development partners is therefore how to help reduce incentives for predation and enhance incentives for more productive use of resources. The issue here is not primarily one of capacity – although weaknesses in state capacity are debilitating, and offer valid entry points for external assistance. Revenue and expenditure management are highly political issues: treating them as purely technical, fiscal questions will lead development partners astray and risks doing harm. The specific support measures outlined below therefore need to be designed and implemented with a view to their impact on state-society bargaining, and their ability to shift the incentives of key stakeholders in constructive ways.

Better management of natural resource revenues and better public financial and macroeconomic management are likely to be high priorities from both a governance and a fiscal perspective, including more effective and consensual resource mobilisation. These are also very legitimate entry points for development partners. Action could include:

Support for domestic measures to control the illicit economy and economic threats to peace, including from illicit trafficking (*e.g.* in narcotics, people, or arms), smuggling (*e.g.* of lootable natural resources), and extortion and capture of state resources. Strategies will need to be context-specific, and may involve a combination of law enforcement, alternative livelihoods provision, curbing regional or global demand, and better management of natural resource revenues.

Support interventions at the global level to reduce opportunities for smuggling, private capture of natural resource rents and money laundering, as well as to increase the transparency of revenues from oil, gas and minerals.

Support measures to strengthen core state monetary and fiscal institutions, including central banks and ministries of finance. Aid delivery mechanisms should aim to strengthen, not undermine, management of public funds.

Support for improved domestic revenue mobilisation, with an emphasis on enhancing equity and voluntary compliance, not just on increasing the overall amounts collected (OECD, 2010a).

Economic development and employment generation

Low levels of economic production and employment also contribute strongly to state fragility; these conditions are usually characterised by particularly low agricultural productivity, little investment in manufacturing and limited entrepreneurial activity in the formal sector. The extent to which states are able to foster growth and employment in these basic productive sectors can become crucial to legitimacy in the eyes of both elites and non-elites, and to state efforts to secure its own revenue base.

In addition to measures discussed above to ensure a minimum level of financial and macroeconomic management, and control the illicit economy, development partners should consider the following.

Restore incentives for productive investment. Investors need confidence that they will be able to earn and retain their profits. In the longer term the goal should be to (re) establish a formal legal framework to support protection of property rights and enforcement of contracts, as well as covering employment, savings and credit.[3] However, relying primarily on best practice approaches to improving the investment climate may be inappropriate in post-conflict, fragile environments, where rent creation and patronage are rife and central to maintaining public order. Efforts to strengthen a formal legal framework may be less effective in the short to medium-term than looking for the potential for politicians and investors to strike bargains that may be informal and exclusive but that build on common interests in security and productive investment (Haber *et al.,* 2003; Qian, 2003; Moore and Schmitz, 2008). Signals from politicians that they will provide investors with protection – either formal or informal – over future profits could be sufficient to kick-start investment. Early measures to restore confidence can send a strong signal to investors and support later stages of the economic recovery process, as shown in Box 2.9.

Box 2.9. **Political signals to investors in Uganda**

After the end of Uganda's civil war in 1986, the Kampala Government took a series of steps to restore and reinforce property rights. This included returning property owned by Asians who had been expelled in 1972. At the time this was a painful measure because the properties concerned had been occupied by local people. However, this approach brought results. In 1986, two-thirds of Ugandan private wealth was held abroad; by the mid-1990s, Uganda was attracting substantial repatriation and this contributed to private sector investment in the country's coffee boom (Collier, 2007).

Prioritise support to rural livelihoods and infrastructure. At the local level, the ways in which people are actually securing their livelihoods needs to be understood. The incentives and constraints they face will be well known to local elites who control whatever minimal productive capacity exists. Understanding these dynamics at local level should be the starting point for any interventions. Often, access to inputs, credit, and marketing opportunities are the greatest challenges faced by farmers and local entrepreneurs. Rural roads (including local roads – not just the highways) are critical not just for access to markets but also for service delivery, and for extending the potential reach of the state.

Provide support to create jobs and ensure that local people, especially women and young people, have appropriate skills and opportunities to enter the labour market. This might include cash-for-work programmes, vocational skills training as long as it is linked to the availability of actual jobs, financial and start-up support for microenterprises, as well as support for small business. Inclusive growth that supports job creation can play a key role in diffusing possible conflict and reducing incentives for people to join criminal or rebel networks. Supporting labour market analyses, skills audits and assessment of economic market opportunities can be an important part of ensuring that initial job creation schemes are translated into sustained employment opportunities.

Target programmes to the most vulnerable populations, including displaced youth and women, to avoid creating further inequities and instability that could undermine the statebuilding process. Short-term measures (*e.g.* social insurance packages or basic living allowances) can help reduce exploitation and exclusion, but should be viewed as part of longer-term strategies to support education, entrepreneurship and livelihoods.

Service delivery

Interventions in service delivery can play a major role in enhancing state legitimacy and contributing to more productive state-society relations and the legitimacy of the state. The provision of basic services that allow for improved access to health care, education, clean water and sanitation are likely to be central to any social contract, alongside basic security and livelihood needs. There are trade-offs between meeting urgent short-term needs and longer-term statebuilding objectives in situations where state capacity is weak, resources are limited, and most services have been degraded through years of neglect

(OECD, 2008c). External actors tend to have inflated expectations of what the state ought to provide and of what external assistance can actually accomplish at reasonable cost in the face of enormous need. Greater realism is needed to help avoid inflated expectations that can undermine statebuilding efforts.

Judgements about how to manage the inevitable trade-offs need to be context-specific. From a statebuilding perspective it is important for the state to have a prominent role in setting the overall legal and policy framework and co-ordinating delivery even if it is not always the direct provider. The question is how to strengthen that role (which itself requires considerable organisational capacity) without damaging existing non-state provision.

Start by mapping state capacity and non-state roles in service provision. Especially where the state is weak, there is likely to be a great diversity of non-state providers filling the gap, with different degrees of co-operation with the state.

Be alert to the risks of using parallel initiatives independent of the state to deliver public services. Such arrangements can divert resources to non-state providers, and set up competing mechanisms. Wherever possible, continue working with the state, for instance using non-state actors to provide services while strengthening the capacity of the state to take responsibility (and be seen to do so) for making policy and contracting, regulating and monitoring services.[4]

Locate partnerships with non-state actors within a budgetary and programmatic framework that emphasises statebuilding, so increasing the potential for all partners to work towards the same priorities in a co-ordinated way and strengthening state capacity for oversight/regulation. Where fiduciary risks are high, consider dual-control oversight mechanisms (OECD, 2010a)

Be mindful of the need to transfer the delivery or oversight of certain services to the state or to decentralised civic or social service agencies at the earliest opportunity. Box 2.10 sets out the approach taken for health services in Afghanistan.

Box 2.10. Government stewardship and NGO delivery of health services in Afghanistan

A situational analysis conducted after the fall of the Taliban demonstrated that the delivery of health services in Afghanistan was very poor. In response to this desperate situation, the Afghan Ministry of Public Health (MoPH): *(i)* established a basic package of health services (BPHS) that prioritised high-impact health interventions; *(ii)* invested heavily in monitoring and evaluation; and *(iii)* contracted with mostly national NGOs to deliver the BPHS using the funds of three major development partners: the World Bank, the United States Agency for International Development, and the European Commission.

Contracting made sense for a number of reasons: NGOs were providing 80% of services being delivered; contracting allowed the MoPH to focus on its stewardship roles (*e.g.* priority setting, co-ordination, monitoring and evaluation); and it allowed for innovative responses to conditions on the ground by the NGOs. By 2008 the health situation looked very different. The experience in Afghanistan indicates that government stewardship is critical but that service delivery by non-state providers can rapidly improve the health situation at community level.

In contexts where state capacity and willingness are low, decentralised service provision is an option. This can help "link up" resilient local communities with local service delivery (OECD, 2008c) and tap into local resources. But there are also risks that interventions financed by development partners will distort or undermine customary, informal institutions, and that decentralisation where the state is weak will encourage further fragmentation of public authority. All these judgements need to be based on the best possible understanding of the local political and institutional context, and a willingness to consider making progress in incremental ways through informal relations of trust between state and non-state providers, as well as formal arrangements (Batley and Mcloughlin, 2010).

Notes

1. Long-term financial and technical assistance can be important, but (as explained in Chapter 4) aid modalities – for example predictability, transparency and use of a country's own systems for channelling and accounting for aid – also help provide incentives and entry points for local collective action.

2. For details, see the Development Assistance Committee Network on Governance (GOVNET) work on taxation.

3. In this regard the OECD Policy Framework for Investment (*www.oecd.org/daf/investment/pfi*) provides a comprehensive framework for domestic governments and donors to guide the design and implementation of policy reform for improving investment conditions in the long term.

4. For a detailed discussion of whether and how to contract out service delivery to non-state providers see OECD (2010b), *Handbook on Contracting Out Government Functions and Services in Post-Conflict and Fragile Situations,* OECD, Paris.

Chapter 3

Choosing tools for analysis and monitoring

This chapter provides an overview of existing tools available to analyse context and invites development partners to (i) *make use of a range of analytical tools to understand the context for statebuilding and* (ii) *understand and monitor external impact on statebuilding and measure progress.*

1. Make use of a range of analytical tools to understand the context for statebuilding

There is a wide range of analytical tools available to support development partner efforts to better understand political context and process, and the factors that help explain state fragility, the potential to support statebuilding and the causes of violent conflict or events that could trigger it. Box 3.1 provides some examples.

Box 3.1. **Tools to analyse context**

- *Political economy analysis* – Political economy approaches focus on the distribution of power and resources in different contexts, with a particular emphasis on informal and formal structures and processes, and the interests, incentives and institutions that support or undermine change. A recent DFID (Department for International Development) How-To Note sets out a range of approaches, including sector-level analysis, that can help explain why reforms in particular sectors (education, health, roads) may have stalled and how development partners might best facilitate change (DFID, 2009). The Dutch Strategic Governance and Corruption Analysis (SGACA) has been specifically adapted for use in fragile states.
- *Problem-driven governance and political economy analysis* – This approach, developed by the World Bank, places the focus on particular challenges or opportunities. A problem-focused approach involves working at three layers: *(i)* identifying the problem, opportunity or specific vulnerability; *(ii)* mapping the institutional and governance arrangements, including weaknesses; and *(iii)* "drilling down to the political economy drivers" to identify obstacles and opportunities for change. This can be applied at country, sector or project level (Fritz, Kaiser and Levy, 2009).
- *Statebuilding impact assessment* – This tool can be used to systematically assess the potential impacts of development partner action on political processes, state-society relations, state legitimacy and social expectations, and the capacity of the state to perform core functions. A template for undertaking an impact assessment can be found in *Do No Harm: International Support to Statebuilding* (OECD, 2010a).
- *Risk assessments* – Risk assessments and analysis enable development partners to uncover the specific risks associated with external support to statebuilding efforts, including political, financial and implementation risks, and to identify how they might impact on each other, and how they are likely to be influenced by different transition contexts. Development partners can then assess the political implications of taking on risks along with specific implications for inaction, and make decisions accordingly on the risks they are able and/or willing to take on.
- *Stakeholder mapping* – A number of tools have been developed to map relevant actors in fragile and post-conflict contexts. Some of these focus on three core types of actors (reformers, preservers and spoilers) that need to be considered at three levels of state-society relations (diaspora, national and sub-national) (Debiel and Terlinden, 2005). This includes state and non-state stakeholders, across formal and informal spheres of political and economic engagement. It also includes both elites and civil society actors.
- *Conflict audits* – An audit approach involves establishing an audit team comprised of representatives from the development partner agency and international and national consultants, to review relevant conflict and political risks. The aim is to produce analyses and country plans, and to prepare a short report that identifies good conflict-sensitive practices and suggests where practices could be improved (DFID, 2010b).

There are large areas of overlap between political economy analysis aimed at understanding the factors driving or inhibiting statebuilding, and analysis aimed at understanding the causes of violent conflict and prospects for peacebuilding – but they have different objectives. The first is particularly valuable in explaining the underlying causes of state fragility; the second provides insights into changes that can destabilise an existing social contract, or trigger or exacerbate violent conflict. In practice, statebuilding and peacebuilding objectives often have to be pursued in parallel, and trade-offs between them reconciled (Chapter 1, p. 47). The Peace and Development Analysis Process has been developed with this in mind (Box 3.2).

Box 3.2. Beyond stand-alone conflict analysis: Peace and development analysis process in Indonesia

While the levels of violence in Indonesia have been dramatically reduced since 2004, several parts of Indonesia are currently in a state of fragile peace. Many of the roots of conflict are still untouched, and while decentralisation and democratisation have provided opportunities for improving accountability and the delivery of services at the local level, they have also created an environment of flux where groups battle for power and resources in a climate of contested and changing rules.

In response to the above challenges, UNDP initiated the Peace and Development Analysis Process (PDA) in partnership with the National Planning Board (Bappenas), the Conflict Studies Centre of the University of Gadja Mada, regional governments and other civil society organisations. The process was aimed at creating safe spaces for dialogue where all relevant, local stakeholders would arrive at a consensus on how to tackle key obstacles to peace and create strategic alliances to work together for the establishment of sustainable peace.

The initial proposal was to undertake a conflict analysis exercise to support the design of UNDP's (and other development partners') responses in three regions affected by conflict. However, a traditional approach to conflict analysis proved inadequate for capturing the complexities of post-conflict dynamics in Indonesia. Thus, consultations with the many stakeholders and an assessment in all three regions led to a radical shift in approach: *(i)* from a conflict to a peace focus; *(ii)* from a project to a process focus; and *(iii)* towards creating mechanisms for peace and development dialogue as an outcome. The PDA is thus an approach that supports dialogue and reconciliation in development planning and programming, aimed not only at formulating a developmental response to post-conflict contexts, but also at addressing the causes of violence and build sustainable peace.

Other elements to bear in mind in using analytical tools include the following.

First, do not focus on assessing problems only but look also at possible drivers of stability and peace. Often, analytical frameworks focus only on problems and assume that by addressing these, capable, accountable, responsive and peaceful states will emerge. However, both statebuilding and peacebuilding experience suggests that analysing current strengths and opportunities can help identify potential solutions and ways forward. These may include, *inter alia,* untapped economic potential, elite fractions that have been sidelined politically, aspects of the national culture, the possibility that significant numbers of educated people might return from the diaspora, and the capacity of women and youth to support effective and sustainable peace.

Second, identify and understand institutional strengths that can help in defining and supporting strategies. Even in the most fragile contexts, functioning institutions and capacity exist. This is not to say that weaknesses and gaps should be ignored, but rather that a balance between the two is required – and looking at strengths is much more empowering than a focus solely on gaps. An example of taking into account existing strengths and capacities was in the development of the Liberian National Capacity Development Strategy, undertaken at the urging of President Sirleaf. The Ministry of Planning and Economic Affairs did considerable diagnostic work, focusing on capacity needs, assets and gaps. The 2006 National Human Development Report for Liberia was both a major analytical input to and an advocate for the strategy (Torori and Reinarz, 2009).

Third, develop a "culture of analysis" within and across the various parts of development partner organisations and governments. Lessons and experiences derived from the development of assessment tools and their implementation suggest that maximising their impact requires a shift from seeing such tools as the driving force in context analysis to building a culture of analysis among and across external actors. This can be done through recruitment and training and by cultivating multiple sources of information and analysis locally and internationally. Development partner staff should be encouraged to "think politically" so that strategies, programmes and day-to-day implementation are regularly informed by contextual information. Assessment tools provide valuable frameworks to guide analysis, and need to be embedded in a wider set of organisational principles and norms about learning and integrating knowledge into practice (Box 3.3).

Box 3.3. Core principles for analysing context

- Encourage development partner staff to "think politically" – hold political analysis team meetings and encourage staff to develop country-specific knowledge as part of their work programme.
- Ensure that analysis has clear operational applicability, including helping to answer defined policy questions, or to formulate questions that require additional investigation.
- Undertake regular analysis requiring tools that are quick and can easily be used again at regular intervals, so that changes and patterns over time can be better understood.
- Analyse your own organisation's actions, motivations and incentives alongside the contexts in which they operate.
- Involve multidisciplinary teams, so that analysis includes political, economic, cultural and social dimensions.
- Involve local expertise such as local consultants and researchers to help inform analysis and understanding of context. Be aware, however, that in some contexts local expertise may not be available, while local actors may not be able to act as "neutral" analysts. This needs to be carefully considered when putting together assessment teams on politically sensitive issues.

Fourth, develop systematic approaches to moving from analysis to strategy and programming priorities. Recent evaluations suggest that despite a strong drive to understand context there has been less systematic attention given to how assessments feed into planning cycles. Ensuring a stronger link between analysis and planning requires that the following take place (IPI, 2009):

- Pay attention to the timing of different parts of this process, and allow for iterations if the context is fluid and uncertain.

- Establish and apply consistent and clear protocols for systematically feeding the results of an assessment into planning or programming.
- Identify opportunities for monitoring and evaluation that are likely to generate evidence or knowledge that inform national processes and political negotiations, or to help capitalise upon economic opportunities.
- Ensure that all parties to these processes are clear about the end-uses and -users of assessments and the way information needs to be presented so as to be readily fed into strategy and planning processes.

2. Understand and monitor external impact on statebuilding, and measure progress

Establishing baselines against which progress can be measured is likely to be imperfect at the outset of any statebuilding or peacebuilding effort. Refinement of goals and establishing the basis for measuring and assessing progress is essential for the accountability of development partner governments toward their political masters and their own parliaments and legislatures. At the same time, defining goals, setting timelines, and establishing performance benchmarks involve political commitments by development partner governments and their partners, as well as by the key political actors within fragile and conflict-affected states. In such a fluid context, the following considerations are pertinent.

First, keep in mind that statebuilding is not a linear process. In a complex and fluid situation it is important to understand change dynamics and how different actors and interventions interact and influence others.

Second, monitor and evaluate the impact of all activities on statebuilding from the beginning and keep adjusting activities as necessary. Establish an environment that is conducive to learning and to the application of knowledge. Monitoring and evaluation should be a real-time activity that contributes to continuous learning and adjustments to strategy and implementation. Tools for effective monitoring and evaluation of interventions, to assess their impact on statebuilding, need to be developed at the analysis stage; these monitoring and evaluation tools should include the collection and analysis of sex-disaggregated and gender-sensitive data (Accra Agenda for Action, 23a) and indicators addressing gender equality and women's empowerment. These should then inform all aspects of analysis, planning and action.

Third, measure and assess progress in terms of statebuilding outcomes over the medium to longer term. Despite the number of tools available, there is no one model for monitoring progress in statebuilding – instead, approaches need to be developed, based on analysis, that are appropriate to context. These should include: *(i)* measures of how sectoral programmes advance statebuilding objectives; *(ii)* measures of transition from fragility to resilience, and/or violent conflict to positive peace; and *(iii)* indicators relating to the three dimensions of the statebuilding process.

As well as linking indicators of progress to country contexts, monitoring and evaluation indicators need to account for the long time frames involved in any fragile or conflict-affected setting and should, where possible, seek to evaluate statebuilding outcomes rather than focus narrowly on activities. Findings from monitoring and evaluation processes should feed back into analysis, so that lessons are systematically included into analysis, planning and action.

Chapter 4

Adapting aid delivery modalities and technical assistance

This chapter discusses how the choice of aid delivery modalities and the delivery of technical assistance impacts statebuilding processes. It invites development partners to align (i) *aid modalities and* (ii) *technical assistance with statebuilding objectives.*

AID DELIVERY

1. Align aid modalities with statebuilding objectives

As noted in previous chapters, development partners face difficult choices between supporting key state functions and meeting urgent needs (essential to state legitimacy), and creating sustainable systems and practices to underpin longer-term state capacity (OECD, 2010a). These decisions are reflected in the choices development partners make between different aid and non-aid instruments at their disposal.

First, understand how aid modalities and other instruments impact (directly or indirectly) on the statebuilding process, and match these modalities to intervention objectives. The main concern is to assess the impact of aid and other forms of support on political processes, legitimacy and state-society relations that are central to statebuilding. Different approaches to aid delivery in fragile contexts can strengthen the state as a centre of decision making and public financial management, or weaken its authority and capacity in this critical sphere.

For example, aid that explicitly avoids state systems may have an adverse impact on future system-strengthening efforts and on the prevailing perceptions of the legitimacy of development partner engagement. Instruments used in humanitarian assistance need to "do no harm" to longer-term statebuilding initiatives: stand-alone project interventions may help to produce quick results but may not serve longer-term statebuilding objectives, in particular when implemented without appropriate partner country participation and co-ordination. Identifying appropriate modalities and approaches will be made easier if it is possible to generate an approximate time frame and sequencing plan, indicating when it may be necessary to transition from short- to longer-term approaches, and how to embed the foundations for longer-term statebuilding in short- to medium-term projects.

Second, in states where the government's legitimacy is in question, or where relations between government and the international community are strained, consider "shadow alignment". "Shadow alignment" is the practice of providing aid in such a way as to mirror national systems, to enable rapid conversion to "real" alignment as soon as conditions permit. Even in the most difficult political contexts, some level of technical dialogue and policy alignment may be feasible with national authorities, for example in basic service delivery. And even where assistance is provided through non-state channels, it can still be delivered in ways that support public sector service delivery, and so avoid undermining the relationship between state and citizen. One function of shadow alignment is providing space for the government to maintain a policy-making and supervisory role over non-state service delivery.

There may be political risks associated with shadow alignment, including providing support to a repressive regime, or allowing a crisis situation to continue by solely addressing its symptoms. The decision-making process over where and how to "shadow align" should involve other diplomatic and security partners to ensure that developmental objectives are in line with agreed political goals and all objectives are mutually reinforcing.

Third, consider the use of jointly managed and pooled funds where appropriate, and adapt them to a changing environment. Jointly managed and pooled funds provide the basis for more aligned and harmonised delivery of assistance. Multi-Donor Trust Funds (MDTFs) have provided an aligned and harmonised approach to financing, in particular in situations where there is lack of state capacity that may prevent direct budget support. MDTFs can also provide a forum for policy dialogue and a joint decision-making process in which partner countries can exercise increasing ownership and leadership. However, MDTFs can often be overambitious in terms of what they can deliver, and cannot always be

Table 4.1. **Opportunities and risks of providing development assistance in fragile contexts**

	Opportunities	Risks
General budget support	Major opportunity to link resources to core capacity building and outcome achievement, while providing incentives to further strengthen country systems. Can finance recurrent expenditure that is central to state functioning. Lower transaction costs for partner country. Joined-up resourcing and dialogue with development partners create a more predictable partner country-development partner relationship.	There may not be a centralised budget to work with. Requires high standards of public financial management to mitigate fiduciary risks. Demanding in terms of the level/type of dialogue with development partners; political objectives and constraints may undermine predictability. Can seem "remote" from short-term improvements in service delivery in the early phases.
Sector budget support	Supports state functioning through an owned sector programme or strategy, while providing incentives to strengthen country systems. Focuses resources on a priority sector. Lower transactions costs than pooled or SWAp-type approaches. Joined-up sector dialogue.	Sector institutions may face particular capacity challenges – for example, with respect to PFM systems. Focused engagement on a priority sector may distort engagement in other key priorities, undermining government decision-making and allocative efficiency.
Government-managed pooled funds	Pooling of development partner resources. Aligned with government strategy, but allows narrower earmarking (often to specific activities) than budget support. Can accommodate safeguard measures where PFM systems are weak.	Earmarking may undermine government's ability to prioritise public investments. Poses management challenges for recipient. Transaction costs may be higher than budget support. Heavy focus on systems and procedures for pooling; decision making can detract from delivering outputs/ outcomes. Pooled funds may delay the transition to budget support when conditions allow.
Jointly managed trust funds (development partner-partner country)	Joint governance and management arrangements mitigate fiduciary risk. Opportunity to develop government systems and capacity for management of resources. Can reduce transaction costs for both development partners and partner countries.	Management challenges for both development partners and partner countries. Attention to improving government systems may in early stages slow down delivery of outputs. Use of trust funds may delay the transition to other aid modalities making greater use of country systems when appropriate.
Project support	Can target specific priorities/gaps, through earmarking for specific activities. Project support can use country systems to differing extents, Flexibility in design. Quick wins.	Can privilege short-term impacts over longer-term engagement. Narrow earmarking can undermine government decision-making and allocative efficiency. Can result in a "dual public sector" and undermine incentives to support state capacity where parallel structures and processes are used. Can create sites of patronage and decision making that rival the state or undermine government processes where parallel structures and procedures are used.
Support to and through non-state actors	Can help to meet short-term service delivery needs where state capacities are weak. Can support citizen engagement and effective channels of participation for marginalised groups. Can foster innovation in service delivery. Flexibility in design. Quick wins.	Can undermine strengthening of government systems. Can undermine transparency and domestic accountability. Can raise social expectations beyond state capacity, fuelling frustration. Can happen in an under-regulated environment.

AID DELIVERY

expected to build state capacity and deliver public goods and services in a timely manner simultaneously. Start-up time and costs are often underestimated and most MDTFs have failed to provide adequate management and technical personnel on the ground. Funds can also be pooled in ways that make fuller use of partner countries' systems. Pooled funds can be used to finance narrowly-defined activities or, as in the case of a sector-wide approach (SWAp), a more comprehensive sector programme.

Fourth, beware of bypassing mainstream government institutions and creating a "dual public sector" (OECD, 2010a). Establishing parallel systems for aid delivery not only undermines long-term capacity and organisational building; it also challenges the very heart of government accountability (Box 4.1). Transferring political and budgetary authority to the host government as soon as practicable is essential for both ownership and accountability. Building key capacities linked to effective budget management and execution helps to achieve service delivery goals and enhance government legitimacy.

Fifth, adopt gradual strategies to deliver sector and general budget support and provide early assistance to build required capacities and safeguards. Sector support approaches have contributed positively to capacity creation within the state and, where done well, have had a positive impact on political processes and state-society relations (OECD, 2010a). Sector-wide approaches (SWAps) provide a context for mixing a range of types of development partner support within a common framework against an agreed set of principles. They can also bring together the work of state and non-state actors, which is vital where capacity is weak or fragmented on the government side (Box 4.2).

Budget support operations, on the other hand, provide an opportunity to consolidate and co-ordinate external partners around a common, government-led programme. This is particularly important during a transition out of conflict, which is often characterised by significant increases in the volume of external assistance, a heavy policy and reconstruction agenda, and limited government capacity to manage external partners effectively. Design of a common budget support programme, backed by a wide range of external partners, can help the government take ownership and assert its leadership of the development agenda, and reduce the risk of policy drift arising from multiple bilateral discussions. It is nevertheless important to be aware of the risks involved and to find ways to mitigate and manage them. Development partners should also establish safeguards to prevent the misuse of funds and to build appropriate capacities to ensure a sustainable and credible management of such programmes.

Sixth, work with civil society actors and find appropriate instruments to channel resources to them. Supporting civil society activities, alongside and outside the state, can be an important counterpart to funding through state mechanisms. These should avoid creating parallel systems but could, for example, support goals such as advocacy for transparency and accountability that generally cannot be achieved if all action is through the state. In general, these funding instruments will contribute more to the development of a proper social contract if they can be used to support relatively small-scale activities. To avoid high transactions costs and, at the same time, avoid creating a grant-based unofficial local bureaucracy, development partners are best advised to channel these funds through international NGOs when these can act with the necessary flexibility and conflict sensitivity.

Seventh, be alert to the timing and predictability of financial flows. Monitor the impact of aid dependency on domestic resource mobilisation. Early investments in economic recovery may not reap immediate rewards; delaying intensive spending until core economic institutions are established is likely to be more effective. Experience from conflict situations suggests that post-conflict cycles tend to affect absorptive capacity

Box 4.1. Project implementation units: Choosing between short-term results and longer-term capacity development

All stakeholders, development partners included, agree that parallel project implementation units represent one of the most problematic areas of development partner practice, creating a parallel public administration system where development partners take decisions on appointments and accounting relationships. Although development partners largely agree that PIUs (project implementation units) are necessary in some fragile situations, particularly in the early recovery stage, their use can lead to exclusion of government from its normal functions – such as in Afghanistan, where an international development partner has almost entirely taken over the Ministry of Defence functions. Because they offer few possibilities for civil society or media oversight, they can also have a negative influence on state-society relations. When they provide services, they can also undermine the relationships between central and local authorities. Despite pledges in the Paris Declaration to reduce parallel PIUs, their numbers are actually increasing in some countries, such as the Democratic Republic of Congo (DRC) where the current number of 146 is four times what it was in 2006. Some development partners have suggested endorsing the formation of PIUs within state ministries as an intermediate measure, but there is fear that this could lead to their deeper institutionalisation.

Box 4.2. SWAps as a positive contribution to statebuilding

The Government of Nepal's "Education For All" programme began in 2004 and will continue until 2009. It focuses on primary education, and uses a pooled fund to finance and manage around 25% of the programme. Denmark, Finland, Norway, DFID, the World Bank, the Asian Development Bank (ADB) and UNICEF support the EFA programme through a joint funding pool that provides sector budget support, earmarked to the overall EFA expenditure programme. Development partners harmonise around a joint financing arrangement (JFA), which commits pooling development partners to "alignment with the budgetary and accountability systems and legislation of Nepal". Development partners have adopted a SWAp to support the Local Governance and Community Development Programme (LGCDP). It will adopt a flexible approach in terms of delivery modalities and include mapping of disadvantaged groups, a social mobilisation approach and public hearings.

In Bolivia, development partners are starting to explore a SWAp in the education ministry. In Rwanda, SWAps have been implemented in the health and education sectors, and now the country is designing the first SWAp in an energy sector anywhere in Africa. In the DRC, development partners note that the ministries responsible for health, education and infrastructure have made much faster progress than other sectors in developing draft sectoral strategies and medium-term budget frameworks. Today, these sectors appear to be receiving more aid to help ministries consolidate their policies and take more ownership of the aid agenda. These programmes all tend to reduce transaction costs in dealing with development partners; build capacity within the state for planning, budget management, monitoring and evaluation; and (often) promote new channels of interaction between social groups and the state. They maintain decision-making processes within the state and therefore have neutral or positive impacts on political processes.

Source: OECD (2010a).

AID DELIVERY

and aid tends to be most effective two to four years after the end of conflict. By contrast, development partners tend to rush in with aid immediately after a conflict and then to pull back flows in the third and fourth years. Delivering too many resources too soon can overwhelm statebuilding efforts in the short run while starving them of critical resources over the medium to long run. Aid inflows can also reduce local tax effort unless equal attention is given to developing national revenue plans as part of national development strategies. Working towards greater predictability through medium-term aid frameworks can create a more stable platform from which to deliver statebuilding support.

2. Align technical assistance with statebuilding objectives

There are many challenges with providing technical assistance (TA), particularly in fragile situations where the very conditions needed to make TA work tend to be weak or absent (*i.e.* reasonable pay levels and working conditions, a modicum of information and management systems, and some processes for the merit-based selection of qualified local personnel). It is also common for TA projects to pepper the entire institutional reform landscape but without much co-ordination and often without much impact. At the same time, if framed and managed properly, technical assistance can not only help restore state functions but also support the development of human resources and contribute positively to the statebuilding process. The following considerations should be taken into account.

First, see TA personnel as an important "ingredient" in developing country capacity but recognise that it can also negatively impact state legitimacy. Development partners need to ensure that this perspective is applied systematically throughout the design, implementation and review of interventions. This includes having a long-term vision of where the TA personnel fit into the change agenda, for example by linking it to locally driven processes of institutional and civil service reform, identifying the kinds of knowledge and techniques to be used and the implications of those choices.

Second, pay more attention to the balance between long-term and short-term technical assistance. Programmes to build state capacity need to be able to rely on long-term technical assistance in their initial phases. To be effective, consultants need time to learn about local conditions, build relationships with public servants and eventually transfer skills. Frequent missions by short-term experts may do harm to statebuilding by placing high demands on overburdened counterparts (OECD, 2010a). Over time, however, a measure of success of technical assistance is the ability of states to eliminate the need for long-term assistance and increasingly identify their own needs for specific short-term expertise.

Third, embed technical assistance in national structures as quickly as possible and develop state capacity to manage TA. When TA personnel are outside of government structures, engagement and ownership by the partner country tend to be low and accountability diffused. Agreeing with national counterparts on the parameters for the delivery of TA may take time. Until then, small, iterative activities are best to give the development partner time to better understand the context and agree with the partner country on where outside assistance can be most useful. Development partners also need to invest more efforts in developing the capacity of state officials to manage technical assistance themselves (OECD, 2010a). This involves creating the capacity to identify the needs for assistance, to consider and choose the consultants to be hired, and to monitor and evaluate their work.

Fourth, balance the need for immediate capacity with efforts to create capacity within the state. This means getting right the combination of (on the one hand) emergency gap-filling actions, which help organisations to respond to political pressures for action, and (on the other) a longer-term focus on transferring skills and developing national capacity such as leadership and management of human resources reforms in government departments. Defining benchmarks to identify the competencies nationals require to take over is helpful as long as these take into account the country context, including the kinds of personnel available (Box 4.3).

Box 4.3. **Transition from "doing" to "supporting" in the Auditor General's office – Solomon Islands**

By 2003, the Office of the Auditor General (OAG) in the Solomon Islands had a staff of three compared to 28 in 1978. Like other accountability institutions it had been starved of funding, and it was critical to restore its authority by sending a clear message that those in public office would be held to account for monies and responsibilities allocated to them. The initial technical assistance supplied by the Regional Assistance Mission to Solomon Islands was focused on direct interventions to clear the backlog of audits and hence send the message. Current TA is more focused on helping Solomon Islands team members to diagnose problems and think through a range of possible solutions. The transition from one to the other was based on an understanding that while the product is important, it is supporting the emergence and consolidation of the process that leads to a product that is likely to hold the key to a resilient and competent OAG.

Source: Bailey (2009).

Fifth, increase the co-ordination of TA by avoiding fragmentation into small projects of excessively short duration and strengthening existing development partner co-ordination mechanisms for TA activities. The latter can be done by establishing groups of "concerned development partners" in charge of facilitating TA co-ordination in specific sectors or organisations, and providing funding with a medium-term perspective and, where appropriate, through pooled funding mechanisms (Michailof, 2007). Finally, co-ordination of TA will improve by transferring task management responsibilities for TA (including monitoring) to the field.

Chapter 5

Improving development partner operations

Development partners will need to strengthen their own capacity and align internal organisational incentives in order to provide effective support to statebuilding in fragile and conflict-affected situations. This chapter recommends that development partners: (i) *strengthen field presence and capacity to work on statebuilding in fragile situations;* (ii) *manage the risks of operating in fragile and conflict-affected situations and learn from failures;* (iii) *create incentives for collaboration and whole of government co-operation;* (iv) *review procedures and regulations in the light of statebuilding objectives;* (v) *be aware how their presence and behaviour affects their legitimacy in the eyes of the local population.*

This chapter sets out a number of operational priorities for working with statebuilding processes in fragile contexts.

1. Strengthen field presence and capacity to work on statebuilding in fragile situations

Fragile contexts are complex and politically sensitive places for development partners to work. Working effectively requires thinking differently about frontline presence and on-the-ground capacity to engage. In the majority of cases this means external actors should consider the following improvements to current practice.

First, devolve greater responsibility to the field. This requires taking into account the increased costs and risks of operating in fragile and conflict-affected contexts, including the cost of staff safety and security, together with the support needed to work effectively in often difficult and changing circumstances.

Second, increase the staff-to-aid spending ratio. Staffing ratios across country programmes are generally calculated according to the size of the aid spent. In fragile contexts this is rarely appropriate given the complexity of the working environment. It is also inappropriate for supporting statebuilding processes given the knowledge base, the range of roles and the longer time frames that staff need to cover compared with more conventional aid programmes. Understanding political processes or the way local networks of power operate requires longer and more specialised commitment by development partner agencies as they mobilise external expertise to implement their programmes.

Third, put incentives in place to attract the best staff to fragile situations, and value country knowledge as well as technical know-how. The statebuilding agenda places a premium on development partner staff thinking politically and being able to engage in a range of facilitative and convening roles. Encourage staff to invest in country knowledge and the development of skill sets consistent with facilitating and managing a wide range of relationships at country level and beyond. This requires the active management of staff turnover through extended assignments and the development of explicit tools and mechanisms for retaining institutional memory (Box 5.1).

Fourth, train staff on the complexities of working in conflict-affected and fragile contexts. Ensure that they have access to, and are trained in the use of practical tools and guidance. Consider joint training across government and with other development partners. Link staff training to a programme of institutional change so agencies are fully fit for purpose in statebuilding in situations of fragility and conflict (Box 5.2).

2. Manage the risks of operating in fragile and conflict-affected situations and learn from failures

The higher risks associated with operating in fragile and conflict-affected situations need to be recognised and actively managed so that they do not become a barrier to staying engaged or to flexible and innovative ways of working. Staying engaged requires a strong understanding of context but also the ability to learn from failures and to adapt programmes to changing circumstances.

First, reward staff for innovation and responding to opportunities; support learning by identifying the practices that contributed to successes and failures. Staff need to be encouraged to seize opportunities when they arise and to propose and pursue innovative ways of working. However, with risk comes failure and it is important that staff are not

Box 5.1. HR incentives to support staff working in fragile settings

A recent survey (Meeting Workforce Demands of Hostile and Difficult Environments) conducted within DFID has resulted in recommendations designed to improve the number and quality of candidates willing to work in such environments. As a result, DFID is:

- Providing staff in the most difficult and important posts with a package of allowances that compensates them appropriately, including for example regular "breather breaks" appropriate to the difficulty of the posting.
- Identifying key "hard to fill" posts well in advance of need and developing a pool of DFID volunteer staff to be considered for suitability. These posts will not be advertised in the same way as other DFID posts and if a DFID volunteer is not selected, the Stabilisation Unit, Civil Service Stabilisation Cadre will be searched for a suitable alternative.
- Exercising flexibility on "next posting" where the candidate takes a particularly difficult post. For example: providing a guarantee of preferred next posting in terms of type of job or geographical location.
- Selecting candidates in external recruitment exercises with the core skills in greatest demand and make first appointment to a difficult post.

Box 5.2. Training staff: The World Bank's Core Operational Policy Course on Fragility and Conflict

The World Bank's Core Operational Policy Course on Fragility and Conflict aims to enhance staff capacity to address the differentiated development needs of fragile and/or conflict-affected countries. The course aims to: increase the ability of staff to diagnose fragile and conflict-affected situations; increase the operational range and focus of the strategic choices country teams make by equipping them with specific tools; strengthen the operational competence of staff to draw on the most appropriate policies, procedures, and programmatic approaches; and improve the capacity of staff to partner with other key actors. The course includes an innovative approach to learning via a simulation exercise, based on the fictional country of *Carana,* which allows participants to "externalise" and test their new knowledge by applying it in practice.

AusAID has recently adapted the course for use with its whole-of-government partners, with the aim of developing a common understanding of the issues and approaches that can be applied to their joint efforts in addressing issues of conflict and fragility in the Asia-Pacific region.

expected to shoulder the burden of risk taking without institutional support. Staff need to be given clear signals of what outcomes they will be held accountable for and evaluated against, how success and failure will be determined, how much risk staff should reasonably take, and how overall performance evaluation ratings and staff career development will take these into account.

Second, share risks by working with other development partner agencies – bilateral and multilateral. Some risks can be shared by working with or through other bilateral and multilateral agencies. Joint development partner offices and joint programming allow for sharing some of the "burden" of working in a risky environment, while pooling arrangements can spread some of the costs of risk mitigation among multiple partners. Other kinds of risks, associated with staff operating in unpredictable and complex environments, can also be managed in tandem with other development partner agencies (Box 5.3).

Box 5.3. **Joint Risk Management Office – Nepal**

After 2001, conditions for the implementation of projects in Nepal deteriorated considerably. Travelling to project locations became much more risky and the pressures increased for an in-country development partner. To respond to the changing situation, the United Kingdom and Germany collaborated to improve their security management by implementing a range of measures to increase personal safety of staff and ensure that development activities could continue. The joint Risk Management Office (RMO) was created in 2002, co-financed by DFID and GTZ. The aim was to keep the office small with one highly qualified external crisis manager, two national experts and some support staff. A network of district emergency co-ordinators and programme staff of DFID and GTZ in different implementing districts supports the RMO and its services. Core activities encompass situational analysis and security-related advisory services to both organisations and their respective projects, training for staff members, and acute crisis management (*e.g.* assistance and guidance following assaults).

Third, communicate better to parliaments and the public about the interests, complexity and long-term nature of supporting statebuilding processes in fragile situations. Maintaining an enabling environment for operations in fragile contexts is important. This requires building a constituency of support for engagement in fragile contexts and with statebuilding processes – particularly by, for example:

- Allocating staff time to gathering lessons and results on statebuilding from country programmes, and translating these into user-friendly communications products.
- Compiling longer-term examples that look back 10-20 years, to show how progress on statebuilding has been achieved over time and supported by development partners.
- Using external scrutiny of development partner programmes in fragile states (*e.g.* by parliamentary committees or national audit offices) as opportunities to explain the importance, nature and challenges of statebuilding work to these stakeholders.

Fourth, adapt to changing circumstances. The development context in fragile situations often changes rapidly. Developing scenarios can inform programme and project development, and can be used as a means to heighten awareness among development partners and agencies of the requirements of joint future action. The Swiss Government has developed an instrument to support the adaptation of country programmes to changing circumstances (Box 5.4).

3. Create incentives for collaboration and whole-of-government co-operation

Fostering coherence and collaboration among the various government departments or institutional groups engaged in situations of fragility and conflict requires setting appropriate incentives within the organisations.

First, strengthen integration and co-operation across departments within your organisation and create incentives for staff to work across departments and with other relevant policy actors. Recognise the value of networking and building informal relationships as central to creating the knowledge base and contacts for working effectively on statebuilding issues. Encourage co-operation across policy communities relevant to operating

Box 5.4. Monitoring of development-relevant changes in circumstances – Switzerland's MERV

In order to better understand changing contexts and thus be in a position to adapt programmes accordingly, the Swiss Government has developed its own instrument for context assessment. The so-called MERV (the German acronym for the monitoring of development-relevant changes in circumstances) is applied in all partner countries with varying frequency; in countries experiencing armed conflict, the frequency is usually between one and three months. MERV assessments are jointly produced by the country teams consisting of development, humanitarian and diplomatic staff at the international and local levels. In some countries, regular local risk assessments complement this standard instrument. Depending on the situational analysis, programming and annual planning are fine-tuned in line with the MERV cycle. During the conflict in Sri Lanka, for example, MERV assessments were grounded in Switzerland's Medium Term Plan 2007-2009 which defined three main scenarios, several sub-scenarios as well as clear exit criterion for Swiss co-operation.

in fragile settings and recognise this co-operation in staff appraisal processes. Ensure that performance assessment systems take into account the different skills required and the difficulty of attributing specific statebuilding results to an individual member of staff, particularly where this has involved joint activities with other departments.

Second, create incentives for country managers and field staff to co-operate rather than compete with other development partners, for example by including co-operation in staff appraisals. Recognise and reward teamwork and encourage the related attitudes and behaviours. Encourage staff to participate in peer review exercises and to solicit feedback from their colleagues within and outside the organisation, including partner country governments and development partners. This will strengthen implementation of mutual accountability, which requires that development partners respond to external evaluations and feedback.

Third, encourage an organisational culture that understands the importance of networks and maximises informal exchange of knowledge and understanding. Promote informal incentives, related to job satisfaction, peer recognition and specific informal rewards. This can be done by: issuing invitations to present at retreats and events; making specific references to groups, teams or individuals in speeches; including specific accomplishments or practices in best practice guidelines or case studies; recognising those who are seen to be at the cutting edge of current practice; and fostering opportunities for the mutual recognition of common efforts with colleagues from partner country governments or development partners.

Fourth, ensure that individual performance assessment systems appropriately reward time and effort spent on building relationships and facilitating change, not just technical quality and fulfilment of disbursement targets. Training, language ability, and the accumulation of country knowledge in relation to fragile contexts could be considered as key elements of future promotion.

4. Review procedures and regulations in the context of statebuilding objectives

Often it is the perception (negative or not) of international engagement – the logos, the branding and the volume of expatriate staff – that shapes local perception of its place and legitimacy in supporting statebuilding efforts. It is therefore important to review procedures and regulations that fuel potentially negative perceptions of international engagement and may negatively impact on statebuilding processes.

First, be mindful of the impact that development partner branding policies can have on statebuilding efforts. In settings where local ownership is fragile and international engagement politically sensitive, logos, flags and project motifs can fuel negative perceptions and ultimately undermine statebuilding efforts. This requires development partners to carefully balance the need for accountability to domestic constituencies with the recognition of a partner government's leadership.

Second, review in-country hiring and procurement procedures to minimise the negative impact and enhance the positive impact on the local labour market and the local economy. This is important anywhere, but in fragile situations where the footprint of any international engagement can be very significant, it is important to avoid aggravating (or creating) market distortions while supporting market development. Not only can development partner agencies and other international actors like NGOs create a brain-drain away from state organisations, but they can also influence wider hiring practices within the state that may be difficult to sustain over time, or to incorporate in sound programmes of civil service reform. Differential salaries paid to those working as consultants and those on civil service wages can create motivational problems, with negative impacts on local perceptions of the international community and on performance and state legitimacy. While procuring and hiring locally constitute a valuable tool for creating job opportunities, stimulating the domestic private sector and reinforcing the legal economic system, it is necessary to adapt hiring and procurement procedures and/or practices to in-country economic and development conditions, in order to ensure that the international engagement does not disadvantage but benefits the local population (Box 5.5).

Box 5.5. NATO's economic footprint project in Afghanistan

Following a request from NATO member states, NATO's Economic Committee has been tasked to undertake an analysis of NATO and International Security Assistance Force (ISAF) nations' "economic footprint" on the Afghan economy. The analysis is currently under way (with support from OECD INCAF) and includes interviews with national representatives in NATO capitals and in the Provincial Reconstruction Teams (PRTs) of six ISAF Troop Contributing Nations – the Czech Republic, Lithuania, the Netherlands, New Zealand, Sweden, and the United States. The analysis will focus on a number of specific questions that impact the local economic footprint, including *(i)* mission structure, *(ii)* procurement practices, *(iii)* hiring and salary practices, *(iv)* activities for building Afghan economic capacities. The study will particularly focus on procurement practices and practices for building capacity in the public and private sectors, with the aim of recommending a pragmatic means by which local procurement could be increased so as to deepen and broaden the positive economic footprint, as well as support economic sustainability and Afghan ownership of development. The goal of the study is to encourage NATO and at a later stage NATO member states to enhance local procurement in Afghanistan.

Third, provide partner countries with complete, accurate and timely information on aid disbursements, with special attention to data on off-budget support. Transparent reporting of aid inflows is important in every context, but in fragile contexts the legacy of lack of transparency and accountability in public financial management gives it particular importance. Given the condition of state bureaucracies and management systems in most fragile contexts, getting aid recorded "on-budget" is a process that needs to be linked to capacity development within the state and improved information systems for budget managers.

Fourth, ensure non-diplomatic foreign personnel abide by the law on local income taxes in their country of residence and applicable international law. Countries could consider subjecting non-diplomatic foreign personnel living and working in fragile and conflict affected contexts to local income taxes. Non-diplomatic staff paying local taxes sets a positive example within the societies of fragile states and, by increasing the local tax base and expanding capacity in revenue authorities, contributes positively to statebuilding.

Fifth, ensure that contractors adhere to guidelines on operating in fragile and conflict-affected situations (using contracts to specify such requirements), and monitor their compliance. Some development partners may decide to develop specific guidelines linked to this guidance on the priority issues and ways of working to be taken into account.

5. Be aware of the impact of your presence and behaviour on your legitimacy

In placing staff in the field it is essential to actively manage the balance between attending to essential security needs and organisational efficiency with presenting an image as a constructive field presence. Invest in ensuring culturally sensitive and context-appropriate behaviour by all staff (Box 5.6.) while paying close attention to the risks to overall effectiveness and working relationships.

Box 5.6. AusAID's Making a Difference programme

AusAID's Making a Difference programme is designed to bring together technical assistance personnel and their country partners in a safe place outside the workplace to give them a shared learning experience on equal terms. The programme aims to empower participants to express their views as their understanding of cultural differences and power imbalances develops. Participants are supported in developing capacity building tools, techniques and experiences to be applied at individual, group and organisational levels. The programme combines learning workshops and back-on-the-job practice. It draws on techniques from mentoring and coaching, change management and process consulting.

According to a 2008 evaluation, the Making a Difference programme has had a significant positive impact on AusAID technical assistance personnel and their partner organisations. Both in the Solomon Islands and in Papua New Guinea, most of the anticipated professional and personal learning objectives were met. The wider impact of the programme was felt in the day-to-day interactions between AusAID partners and their colleagues in the Papua New Guinea public service, and it was extended beyond the participants to a broader group of government officials and advisers through the community of practice.

Source: OECD (2009b).

OPERATIONS

Bibliography

Anten, Louise, Mariska van Beijnum and Leontine Specker (2009), "3C Approaches to Fragile and Conflict Situations – Taking Stock of Commitments and Challenges", Netherlands Institute of International Relations, Clingendael.

Bailey, Laura (2009) "Building Post-Crisis Capacity: Cases from the Solomon Islands", Capacity Development Brief, No. 32, World Bank, Washington, DC.

Barkey, Karen and Sunita Parikh (1991), "Comparative Perspectives on the State", *Annual Review of Sociology*, Vol. 17, pp. 523-49.

Baser, Heather *et al.* (2008), "Capacity, Change and Performance: A Study", Discussion paper, No. 59B, European Centre for Development Policy Management Discussion.

Batley, Richard and Claire Mcloughlin (2010), "Engagement with Non-State Service Providers in Fragile States: Reconciling State-Building and Service Delivery", *Development Policy Review*, 28 (2), pp. 131-154.

Bellina, Séverine, Dominique Darbon, Stein Eriksen and Ole Jacob Sending (2009), "The Legitimacy of the State in Fragile Situations", Report prepared for the OECD DAC International Network on Conflict and Fragility.

Berger, Mark (2006), "From Nation-Building to State-Building: The Geopolitics of Development, the Nation State System and the Changing Global Order", *Third World Quarterly*, Vol. 27, No. 1, pp. 5-25.

BMZ (Federal Ministry for Economic Cooperation and Development) (2009), "Promoting Resilient States and Constructive State-Society Relations – Legitimacy, Transparency and Accountability", BMZ, Berlin.

Bray, John (2007), "The Role of Private Sector Development in Post-Conflict Economic Recovery", UNDP, New York.

Brinkerhoff, Derick W. (2007a), "Capacity Development in Fragile States", European Centre for Development Policy Management (ECDPM), Discussion paper, No. 58D.

Brinkerhoff, Derick W. (2007b), "Dilemmas and Directions: Capacity Development in Fragile States", *Capacity.Org,* Issue 32.

Brinkerhoff, Derick W. and Ronald Johnson (2008), "Good Enough Governance in Fragile States: The Role of Centre-Periphery Relations and Local Government", Paper presented at the 4th International Specialised Conference on International Aid and Public Administration, International Institute of Administrative Sciences, Ankara, Turkey, 23-27 June.

Brinkerhoff, Derick W. *et al.* (2009), "Guide to Rebuilding Governance in Stability Operations: A Role for the Military?", Peacekeeping and Stability Operations Institute.

Brown, Stephen and Grävingholt Jörn (2009), "Framing Paper on Political Settlements in Peacebuilding and Statebuilding", OECD INCAF framing paper.

Call, Charles (2008), "Conclusion: Building States to Build Peace?" in Charles T. Call with Vanessa Wyeth (eds.), *Building States to Build Peace*, Lynne Rienner Publishers, Boulder.

Call, Charles and Elizabeth Cousens (2007), "Ending Wars and Building Peace", CWC Working Paper Series, International Peace Academy, New York.

Carillo, Susana (2007), "Assessing Governance and Strengthening Capacity in Haiti", Capacity Development Brief, No. 25, World Bank Institute, Washington, DC.

Carment, David, John Gazo and Stewart Prest (2007), "Risk Assessment and State Failure", *Global Society*, Vol. 21, No. 1, pp. 47-69.

Carnahan, Michael and Clare Lockhart (2008), "Peace-Building and Public Finance" in Charles T. Call with Vanessa Wyeth (eds.), *Building States to Build Peace*, Lynne Rienner Publishers, Boulder.

Carothers, Thomas (2007), "The 'Sequencing' Fallacy", *Journal of Democracy*, Vol. 18, No. 1.

Clements, Kevin (2008), "Traditional, Charismatic and Grounded Legitimacy", Study prepared for the GTZ advisory project on "Good Governance and Democracy".

Cliffe, Sarah and Nick Manning (2008), "Practical Approaches to Building State Institutions" in Charles T. Call with Vanessa Wyeth (eds.), *Building States to Build Peace*, Lynne Rienner Publishers, Boulder.

Collier, Paul (2007), *The Bottom Billion: Why the Poorest Countries Are Failing and What Can Be Done About It*, Oxford University Press, Oxford.

Collier, Paul, Anke Hoeffler and Dominic Rohnerz (2008), "Beyond Greed and Grievance: Feasibility and Civil War", Oxford Economic Papers, No. 61.

Collier, Paul and Nicolas Sambanis (2002), "Understanding Civil War: A New Agenda," *Journal of Conflict Resolution*, Vol. 46, No. 1, pp. 3-12.

Cox, Marcus and Cristina Hemon (2009), "Engagement in Fragile Situations: Preliminary Lessons from Donor Experience – A Literature Review", DFID, London.

Cox, Marcus and Nigel Thornton (2009), "DFID Engagement in Countries in Fragile Situations: A Portfolio Review", Synthesis report, DFID, London.

Crook, Richard (2003), "Decentralisation and Poverty Reduction in Africa: The Politics of Local-Central Relations in Africa", *Public Administration and Development,* Vol. 23, No. 1, pp. 77-88.

Debiel, Tobias and Ulf Terlinden (2005), "Promoting Good Governance in Post-Conflict Societies", Discussion paper, Technische Zusammenarbeit, GTZ, Eschborn.

Development Initiatives (2009), "Mapping of Transition Financing Procedures and Mechanisms", Revised draft report, SIDA and DFID on behalf of the INCAF Task Team on Financing and Aid Architecture.

DFID (United Kingdom Department for International Development) (2009), "Political Economy Analysis: How-to Note", Practice paper, DFID, London.

DFID (2010a), "Building Peaceful States and Societies: A DFID Practice Paper", DFID, London.

DFID (2010b), "Working Effectively in Conflict-Affected and Fragile Situations", Briefing paper, No. 2, DFID, London.

Dwan, Renata (2008), "The DRC's Country Assistance Framework: A 'Big Tent' built from 'Big Ideas'?" Joint UN-Bank Review of the DRC CAF.

Fritz, Verena, Kai Kaiser and Brian Levy (2009), *Problem-Driven Governance and Political Economy Analysis – Good Practice Framework*, World Bank, Washington, DC.

Fritz, Verena and Alina Rocha-Menocal (2007a), "Understanding State-Building from a Political Economy Perspective: An Analytical and Conceptual Paper on Processes, Embedded Tensions and Lessons for International Engagement", Report prepared for DFID's Effective and Fragile States Teams.

Fritz, Verena and Alina Rocha-Menocal (2007b), "Developmental States in the New Millennium: Concepts and Challenges for a New Aid Agenda", *Development Policy Review*, Vol. 25, No. 5.

Ghani, Ashraf and Clare Lockhart (2008), *Fixing Failed States: A Framework for Rebuilding a Fractured World*, Oxford University Press, Oxford.

Ghani, Ashraf, Clare Lockhart and Michael Carnahan (2005), "Closing the Sovereignty Gap: An Approach to State-Building", Working paper, No. 253, Overseas Development Institute, London.

Goldstonc, Jack (2008), "Pathways to State Failure", *Conflict Management and Peace Science*, Vol. 25, pp. 285-296.

Grävingholt, Jörn, Stefan Gänzle and Sebastian Ziaja (2009), "The Convergence of Peacebuilding and State Building: Addressing a Common Purpose from Different Perspectives", Briefing paper, No. 4, German Development Institute (DIE), Hamburg.

Grindle, Merilee (2007), "Good Enough Governance Revisited", *Development Policy Review*, Vol. 5, No. 25, pp. 533-574.

GTZ (Deutsche Gesellschaft für Technische Zusammenarbeit) (2008), *State-Building in the Context of Fragile Statehood and Poor Government Performance: Lessons Learnt by German Development Cooperation*, GTZ, Eschborn.

Haber, Stephen, Armando Razo and Noel Maurer (2003), *The Politics of Property Rights Political Instability, Credible Commitments and Economic Growth in Mexico, 1876-1929,* Cambridge University Press, Cambridge.

Hudson, Alan (2009), "Background Paper for the Launch of the Workstream on Aid and Domestic Accountability", Network on Governance (GOVNET), OECD DAC, Paris.

IPI (International Peace Institute) (2009), "Understanding Local Context: The Use of Assessment Tools for Conflict Affected and Fragile States", International Peace Institute, New York.

Islamic Republic of Afghanistan (2009), "Government of the Islamic Republic of Afghanistan Civilian Technical Assistance Plan", Islamic Republic of Afghanistan, Kabul.

Kaltenborn-Stachau, Henriette von (2008), "The Missing Link: Fostering Positive Citizen-State Relations in Post-Conflict Environments", Communication for Governance & Accountability Program (CommGAP), World Bank, Washington, DC.

Kusek, Jody Z. and Ray C. Rist (2004), *Ten Steps to a Results-Based Monitoring and Evaluation System*, World Bank, Washington DC.

LSE/PWC (London School of Economics and PricewaterhouseCoopers) (2009), "Statebuilding in Fragile Situations – How Can Donors 'Do No Harm' And Maximise Their Positive Impact? Country Case Study – Sierra Leone", Joint study prepared for OECD INCAF by LSE and PWC.

Mann, Michael (1984), "The Autonomous Power of the State: Its Origins, Mechanisms and Results", *Archives européennes de sociologie,* Vol. 25, pp. 185-213.

Marshall, Thomas Humphrey (1950), *Citizenship and Social Class, And Other Essays*, Cambridge University Press, Cambridge.

Michailof, Serge (2007), "Review of Technical Assistance and Capacity Building in Afghanistan", Discussion paper for the Afghanistan Development Forum.

Migdal, Joel (2001), *State in Society: Studying How States and Societies Transform and Constitute One Another*, Cambridge University Press, Cambridge.

Moore, Mick (2004), "Revenues, State Formation, and the Quality of Governance in Developing Countries", *International Political Science Review,* Vol. 25, No. 3.

Moore, Mick, Anna Schmidt and Sue Unsworth (2009), "Assuring Our Common Future in a Globalised World: The Global Context of Conflict and State Fragility", DFID background paper for the 2009 White Paper "Securing our Common Future".

Moore, Mick and Hubert Schmitz (2008), "Idealsim, Realism and the Investment Climate in Developing Countries", Working Paper. No. 307, Institute of Development Studies, Brighton.

Morgan, Peter (2009), "Some Findings on Donor Support to Capacity Development in Two Post-Conflict States", World Bank, Washington, DC.

OECD (2006a), *The Challenge of Capacity Development: Working Towards Good Practice*, OECD DAC, Paris.

OECD (2006b), "Whole of Government Approaches to Fragile States", OECD DAC Guidelines and Reference Series, DAC reference report, OECD DAC, Paris.

OECD (2007a), *OECD DAC Handbook on Security System Reform,* OECD DAC, Paris.

OECD (2007b), "Principles on Good International Engagement in Fragile States and Situations", OECD DAC, Paris, *www.oecd.org/dataoecd/61/45/38368714.pdf.*

OECD (2008a), "Concepts and Dilemmas of State-Building in Fragile Situations: From Fragility to Resilience", OECD/DAC Discussion Paper, OECD DAC, Paris.

OECD (2008b), *Governance, Taxation and Accountability: Issues and Practices,* DAC Guidelines and Reference Series, OECD DAC, Paris.

OECD (2008c), *Service Delivery in Fragile Situations: Key Concepts, Findings and Lessons*, OECD, Paris.

OECD (2008d), "State Building in Situations of Fragility: Initial Findings", OECD DAC, Paris.

OECD (2009a), *Armed Violence Reduction: Enabling Development,* OECD DAC, Paris.

OECD (2009b), "Donor Capacity Development Innovation: Australia", Issues Brief, No. 5, OECD DAC, Paris.

OECD (2010a), *Do No Harm: International Support to Statebuilding*, OECD DAC, Paris.

OECD (2010b), *Handbook on Contracting Out Government Functions and Services in Post-Conflict and Fragile Situations,* OECD, Paris.

OECD (2010c), *The Legitimacy of the State in Fragile Situations*, OECD DAC, Paris.

Ogbaharya, Daniel (2008), "(Re)building Governance in Post-Conflict Africa: The Role of the State and Informal Institutions", Development in Practice, Vol. 18, pp. 395-402.

Papagianni, Katia (2008), "Participation and State Legitimation" in Charles T. Call with Vanessa Wyeth (eds.), *Building States to Build Peac*e, Lynne Rienner Publishers, Boulder.

Paris, Roland (2004), *At War's End: Building Peace after Civil Conflic*t, Cambridge University Press, Cambridge.

Paris, Roland and Timothy Sisk, eds. (2008), *The Contradictions of State Building: Confronting the Dilemmas of Post-War Peace Operations,* Routledge, London.

Patrick, Stewart and Kaysie Brown (2007), *Greater than the Sum of Its Parts: Assessing "Whole of Government" Approaches to Fragile States*, International Peace Academy, New York.

Pradhan, Sanjay (2009), "Building Capacity to Move Past Conflict and Fragility – An Agenda for Action", *Development Outreach,* World Bank Institute, pp. 6-9.

Putzel, James (2007), "Governance Challenges in Post-War States: Security, Democratic Politics and Economic Management", Crisis States Research Centre, LSE. Paper presented at the "Engaging with Fragile States: Challenges and Opportunities" Conference, Addis Ababa, 24 July, *www.worldbank.org/ieg/licus/conference/presentations/James_Putzel.pdf.*

Qian, Yingyi (2003), "How Reform Worked in China" in Rodik, Dani (ed.), *In Search of Prosperity: Analytic Narratives on Economic Growth,* Princeton University Press, Princeton, NJ.

Rocha-Menocal, Alina and Verena Fritz (2008), "Hybrid Regimes and the Challenges of Deepening and Sustaining Democracy in Developing Countries", *South African Journal of International Affairs,* Vol. 15, No. 1, pp. 29-40.

Rocha-Menocal, Alina and Bhavna Sharma (2008), "Joint Evaluation of Citizens' Voice and Accountability: Synthesis Report", DFID, London.

Sardesai, Shonali and Per Wam (2006), "Effective Conflict Analysis Exercises: Overcoming Organisational Challenges", World Bank/IRDB document.

Schedler, Andreas (1999), "Conceptualizing Accountability" in Andreas Schedler Larry Diamond and Marc F. Plattner (eds.) *The Self-Restraining State: Power and Accountability in New Democracies*, Lynne Rienner Publishers, Boulder.

Sisk, Timothy and Vanessa Wyeth (2009), "Rethinking Peace-Building and State-Building in War-Torn Countries: Conceptual Clarity, Policy Guidance, and Practical Implications", Draft discussion note for the OECD DAC International Network on Conflict and Fragility.

Smutylo, Terry (2005), "Outcome Mapping: A Method for Tracking Behavioural Changes in Development Programs", ILAC brief, The Institutional Learning and Change Initiative – hosted by the International Plant Genetic Resources Institute.

Snyder, Jack (2000), *From Voting to Violence: Democratization and Nationalist Conflict*, Norton Books, New York.

Sogge, David (2006), "Angola: Global 'Good Governance' Also Needed", Working paper, No. 23, FRIDE, Madrid.

Steans, Jill (2006*), Gender and International Relations: Issues, Debates, and Future Directions*, Polity Press, Cambridge.

Stewart, Frances (ed.) (2008) *Horizontal Inequalities and Conflict: Understanding Group Violence in Multiethnic Societies,* Palgrave Macmillan, Houndsmills.

Stewart, Frances and Graham Brown (2006), "Fragile States", Policy paper, Centre for Research on Inequality, Human Security and Ethnicity (CRISE), *www.crise.ox.ac.uk/pubs/workingpaper51.pdf.*

Tilly, Charles (1985), "War Making and State Making as Organized Crime" in Peter Evans (ed.), *Bringing the State Back In*, Cambridge University Press, Cambridge.

Tilly, Charles (1990), *Coercion, Capital, and European States, AD 990-1992,* Blackwell Publishing, Malden.

Tisne, Martin, Karen Hussmann and Harald Mathiesen (2009), "Integrity in Statebuilding: Anti-Corruption with a Statebuilding Lens", Background Paper for the OECD DAC Network on Governance, OECD DAC, Paris.

Torori, Cleophas and Lisa Reinarz (2009), "Making Capacity Development Work in a Post-Conflict Context: Experience and Lessons Learnt in Liberia", *Africa ViewPoint*, No. 14, UNDP Regional Bureau for Africa.

UNDP (United Nations Development Programme) (2008), "Crisis Prevention and Recovery Report: Post-Conflict Economic Recovery, Enabling Local Ingenuity", UNDP, New York.

UNDP (2009), "A User's Guide to Measuring Gender-Sensitive Basic Service Delivery," UNDP, New York.

UNDP/USAID (United States Agency for International Development) (2007), "First Steps in Post-Conflict State-Building: A UNDP-USAID Study", USAID, Washington, DC.

UNDPKO (United Nations Department of Peacekeeping Operations) (2008), *United Nations Peacekeeping Operations Principles and Guidelines,* Department of Field Support, UNPKO, New York.

UNIFEM (United Nations Development Fund for Women) (2008/2009), *Who Answers to Women? Gender and Accountability*, Progress of the World's Women Report.

Weber, Max (1968), *Economy and Society,* Bedminster Press Incorporated, New York.

Whaites, Alan (2008), "States in Development: Understanding State-Building", Working Paper, DFID, London.

Wolpe, Howard and Steve McDonald (2008), "Democracy and Peace Building: Rethinking the Conventional Wisdom", *In the Round Table,* Vol. 97, No. 394, pp. 137-145.

World Bank (2006), "Engaging with Fragile States: An IEG Review of World Bank Support to Low-Income Countries under Stress", World Bank, Washington, DC.

World Bank, EC, AfDB (European Commission, African Development Bank) (2008), "Coordination on Bugdet Support in Fragile States, A Common Approach Paper", Concept note, World Bank, European Commission, African Development Bank.

World Bank/International Bank for Reconstruction and Development (2007), *Tools for Institutional, Political and Social Analysis of Policy Reform: A Sourcebook for Development Practitioners*. Vol. 19, No. 2, World Bank, Washington, DC.

ORGANISATION FOR ECONOMIC CO-OPERATION AND DEVELOPMENT

The OECD is a unique forum where governments work together to address the economic, social and environmental challenges of globalisation. The OECD is also at the forefront of efforts to understand and to help governments respond to new developments and concerns, such as corporate governance, the information economy and the challenges of an ageing population. The Organisation provides a setting where governments can compare policy experiences, seek answers to common problems, identify good practice and work to co-ordinate domestic and international policies.

The OECD member countries are: Australia, Austria, Belgium, Canada, Chile, the Czech Republic, Denmark, Estonia, Finland, France, Germany, Greece, Hungary, Iceland, Ireland, Israel, Italy, Japan, Korea, Luxembourg, Mexico, the Netherlands, New Zealand, Norway, Poland, Portugal, the Slovak Republic, Slovenia, Spain, Sweden, Switzerland, Turkey, the United Kingdom and the United States. The European Commission takes part in the work of the OECD.

OECD Publishing disseminates widely the results of the Organisation's statistics gathering and research on economic, social and environmental issues, as well as the conventions, guidelines and standards agreed by its members.

OECD PUBLISHING, 2, rue André-Pascal, 75775 PARIS CEDEX 16
(43 2011 03 1 P) ISBN 978-92-64-07496-5 – No. 57933 2011